DATE DUE			

UNDERSTANDING
MODERN ARCHITECTURE

UNDERSTANDING
MODERN ARCHITECTURE

GEORGE BARFORD

DAVIS PUBLICATIONS, INC.
WORCESTER, MASSACHUSETTS

FOR RUTH ALWAYS,

AND FOR GEORGE, SUSAN, DAVID AND MICHAEL

FOR THEIR INTEREST AND SUPPORT.

Printed in the United States of America

Library of Congress Catalog Card Number: 86-070903

ISBN: 0-87192-179-0

Graphic Design: Outside Designs

Photographs by the author except where noted

Front Cover: *Notre-Dame-du-Haut Chapel,*
Ronchamp, France. Le Corbusier.

Frontis: *Phoenix Mutual Life Insurance Tower,*
Hartford, Connecticut. Harrison and Abramovitz.

Back Cover: *Winter Garden and Rainbow Center Mall,*
Niagara Falls, New York. Gruen Associates, Cesar Pelli.

10 9 8 7 6 5 4 3 2 1

CONTENTS

INTRODUCTION

Architecture is the most lasting and apparent of all arts. After thousands of years, the Pyramids of Egypt and the Parthenon of Greece remain among the wonders of the world. Today, we have imposing giants such as World Trade Center in New York and smaller jewels such as the Chapel at Ronchamp. And like their ancient counterparts, the outstanding examples of Modern Architecture inspire our wonder at how they transform empty space into the ultimate union of form and function.

In the past 150 years or so, many new building styles have appeared. The progressive development of new building materials—iron and steel, reinforced concrete, glass and plastic—has opened up tremendous design possibilities. These new materials along with new construction techniques have spawned a variety of vivid and sometimes shockingly different shapes. Cubes, cones, cylinders, pyramids, spheres dominate the geometry of the urban landscape. Architects are almost unlimited in the number of possible combinations of these forms. Some of the resulting designs are successful, some are not. Some buildings simply "work." Others, though ostensibly similar, are but inferior stylistic imitations.

Evaluating the Modern Architecture so pervasive in our world demands a look back at its roots, at the latter part of the 19th century when architects as well as engineers pioneered buildings and bridges forged in iron and concrete, a radical innovation at the time. In tracing the path of Modern Architecture from then until now, this book examines many of the finest modern buildings and the architects who designed them.

1

INTRODUCTION TO ARCHITECTURE

HOW IT BEGAN

From our knowledge of prehistoric people, we assume that their first shelter was found in caves. After shelter came art, as seen in the wonderful painted caves at Altamira in Spain and Lascaux in France. In some areas, soft rock formations lent themselves to easy digging. People began to dig homes for themselves in the sides of cliffs in Spain, in Sicily, and in the Göreme Valley in Turkey. Gradually simple buildings were developed, such as huts and tents in warm and moderate climates, and igloos in the arctic.

Other early shelters were the clay houses of Mali, Chad and Upper Volta in Africa, the pueblos of Mesa Verde in the Americn southwest, the oval houses of the Maya in Yucatan. There were the leather wigwams of the Plains Indians, the large grass structures of New Guinea, and the felt yurts of the Asian Nomads. With the coming of agriculture, fields had to be cleared of rocks. The rocks were piled up first for fences and later for shelters, which led to such intriguing forms as the trulli of Italy and the nuraghi of Sardinia.

As civilization progressed, people learned to cut and shape stone and created simple stone buildings. Master masons became engineers. Over the centuries marvelous buildings came into being in Egypt and Mesopotamia. The great Egyptian buildings were not city halls or palaces, but tombs, because the afterlife was of supreme importance in the Egyptian religion. About 1500 B.C. Stonehenge was built on Salisbury Plain in England, and the dolmen and menhirs of Cornwall and Brittany were erected. Technically these are not architecture, but they are very interesting structures.

Cave dwellings, Göreme Valley, Turkey. Photograph by Ruth Barford.

Dwellings, Mesa Verde National Park, Colorado. Photograph by Ruth Barford.

Trulli, modern dwellings of ancient heritage, Adriatic Coast, Italy.

1

Some of the most beautiful architecture of antiquity belongs to fifth century B.C. Greece—the Parthenon on the Acropolis, the enchanting temples at Sounion and Aegina, and the temples at Paestum and Agrigento in Italy. Early in the Christian era appeared the great pyramids of Mexico—the Pyramid of the Sun at Teotihuacan, the House of the Magician at Uxmal, the Temple of Kukulkan at Chichen-Itza, the tombs at Monte Alban and Mitla. Splendid early buildings were built at Cuzco and Machu Picchu in Peru, and in India the Great Stupa at Sanchi was begun in 10 B.C. Distinctive shrine architecture was developed in China and Japan as early as the third century A.D. In Cambodia the now world-famous city of Angkor Wat was built early in the twelfth century A.D.

A "Ginna," a house of the Dogon Tribe, Mali. Photograph by Aldo van Eyck.

Stonehenge, Salisbury Plain, England. About 1500 B.C. Photograph by Claire Golding. The circle of immense monoliths at Stonehenge may have been built as an astronomical observatory. Stonehenge is Britain's earliest example of post-and-beam architecture.

Pyramid of the Sun, Teotihuacan, Mexico. Before 800 A.D. The Pyramid of the Sun is an impressive construction well over 200 feet high, with a base of over 700 feet to a side. It is the largest such structure in the Western Hemisphere.

Temple of Kukulkan, Chichen Itza, Yucatan. 12th century.

Shinto Shrine at Ise, Japan. *Characteristics of Shinto shrine architecture of the pre-Buddhist period were asymmetry, an irregular ground plan and a close relationship to the natural site. The thatched roofs are made of very thin sheets of cryptomeria bark, put down in thick layers.*

BASIC MATERIALS

In temperate climates wood has been the most common material for building. It is readily available, easily worked, pleasant to look at, reasonably priced. Log cabins were common in Scandinavia and many parts of the U.S. and Canada. Even today the **balloon frame** of two-by-fours is the standard structure for most American houses.

In desert areas where wood is scarce, builders often have used adobe bricks or whole walls of dried mud. The adobe dwellings of the southwestern United States often are consolidated into pueblos. The Dogon tribe in Mali, Africa, has built some unusual mud houses and granaries.

Where wood was scarce and adobe impractical, builders became masons and built with stone, even if the stone, in many cases, had to be brought long distances. Some common building stones are limestone, sandstone, marble and granite.

After wood, mud and stone, brick is the oldest of building materials. Brick and ceramics were probably discovered accidentally, as clay-lined baskets were burned in a fire. The Roman builders were fond of bricks; witness the Pantheon, the Trajan Forum, and many other Roman buildings. Brick was in use long before the Christian era. It is fireproof and weathers well, so it is very much in use today.

The Romans gave us a good part of Western language and law. Another great legacy was concrete. Think how changed the face of the earth would be if we didn't have concrete. Concrete is a versatile material, strong, durable, and easy to cast in a variety of shapes. It can be manufactured nearly everywhere, and, when reinforced, it is light for its strength.

Iron is one of the youngest of our building materials, although it has been used in other ways for centuries. Its uses in building are dealt with at length in Chapter Two. After iron came steel, which is iron made stronger and more flexible by the addition of carbon or tungsten or vanadium, among other materials. Gustave Eiffel used iron in his splendid bridges and his Paris tower; today contemporary builders would be lost without steel.

Glass can be made by melting together sand and borax. This discovery proved a great boon to builders. Architects were timid at first, using glass only in small punched windows. Now some observers feel that architects have gone to the other extreme. The John Hancock Tower in Boston and the Crystal Cathedral in Garden Grove, California are examples of all-glass facades.

Cloth and other sheet material has been used for a long time to build shelters, from the oval yurts of central Asia to the large tents we use today. With the twentieth century came the development of plastics of various types, styrene, vinyl, and acrylics, among others. Engineers such as R. Buckminster Fuller and Frei Otto have combined steel frameworks with acrylic sheets to form large steel-and-plastic structures. Fuller's Montreal Expo '67 sphere was a spectacular example, as is Frei Otto's 1972 Olympic buildings. Vinyl as a plastic sheet material is sometimes used as a flexible roof supported by blown air to create buildings for storage and other uses.

Shelters can be made out of almost anything, from the flattened gasoline cans and cardboard in the *favelas* of impoverished Brazilians to the walls of polished marble in the condominiums of the wealthy. Dwellers in warm or temperate climates hardly think of snow as a building material, but the Eskimos of the high Arctic use it all the time. Their igloos are often large and surprisingly warm, considering that the walls are of snow.

STRUCTURAL METHODS

The most common construction method, and perhaps the simplest, is the **post-and-beam.** Most buildings past and present have been built with this method. Erect a row of stone or wooden posts on each side of a flat foundation, add roof rafters to span them, and you have the basic box; the roof can be made of a variety of materials.

Temple of Aphaea, *Aegina, Greece. The simplest and most common method of construction is the post-and-beam, or post-and-lintel. Here, stone lintels rest on stone columns in the Temple of Aphaea. In modern construction, steel posts are erected to support long steel beams.*

Following post-and-beam came the arch. The Egyptians and the Greeks didn't have it, and with their wonderful buildings didn't need it. The Maya would have liked it, but they couldn't make a true arch, so they used a **corbeled arch** instead. The Romans developed the **true arch,** and used it well in their buildings and aqueducts.

The Romans also invented the **dome,** which can be beautiful, as in Hagia Sophia, or boring, as in all the county courthouses across America. Walter Gropius once said that the true "International Style" was found in government buildings throughout the Western Hemisphere, with their Corinthian columns and Renaissance domes. Buckminster Fuller made his fame and fortune, and rightfully so, with his geodesic domes. Our most spectacular domes today are the giant sports arenas.

Nunnery Quadrangle, *Uxmal, Yucatan. A corbeled arch is constructed by overlapping inwardly the rows of stones on each side until there is only a small gap at the top, which is closed by a flat cap-stone and the wall continued above it.*

Metro Subway, *Washington, D.C. Harry Weese, architect. The barrel vault, sometimes called the tunnel vault resembles a cylinder cut in half at the ends. It has been used as a building method since early times.*

University of Illinois Assembly Hall, *Champaign. Designed by Max Abramowitz. The dome is an ancient construction method. Byzantine domes were made of carefully cut stone. Some modern sports domes have roofs of plastic sheeting. This dome is of poured concrete. It has hundreds of miles of steel wire wrapped around the outer edge.*

The **Gothic arch** is the one with which we are most familiar; nearly all the famous churches of the West have Gothic arches and vaulting. If the center part of a Romanesque arch were removed and the remains of the two sides moved together, a Gothic or pointed arch would result, the type that is seen in Chartres, Salisbury and Cologne cathedrals.

An outgrowth of the true arch was the **barrel vault,** which can be envisioned as a long row of arches touching one another. The barrel vault is the heart of Romanesque architecture, and if a transept is present a cross-vault results, adding to the beauty of the structure. Of barrel vaults, Vezelay in France is a good example of twelfth century Romanesque, and the St. Louis Airport by Minoru Yamasaki is a modern example.

Cathedral of Reims, *France. Photograph by Michael Barford. The gothic arch is a pointed arch which gave birth to spectacular vaulting, allowing for large window spaces and much needed light in the interior.*

Roman Aqueduct, *Segovia, Spain. Photograph by Richard Hentz. The Romans developed the round arch into a thing of beauty and used it in a majority of their buildings. Built over wooden forms, the arches have wedge-shaped voussoir stones which spring from the top of each column and are held in place by a keystone in the center.*

Another kind of arch is the **catenary arch,** such as the Jefferson Memorial Arch in St. Louis. Its designer, architect Eero Saarinen, arrived at the near-parabolic curve by hanging a chain from two points until the resulting curve satisfied him. Antonio Gaudi used the same method in designing his chapel for the Colonia Güell. The catenary curve is sometimes used in hanging cables to support a roof, as in Dulles Airport near Washington or in Tokyo's Olympic Stadium.

A basic structure found often in nature but less often in architecture is the hyperbolic paraboloid, or hypar for short. The outstanding contemporary designer using hypars is Felix Candela, formerly of Mexico, now of the U.S. His churches in Mexico combine strength and delicacy.

Tent structures have existed for centuries, but skilled and imaginative engineers such as Frei Otto of Germany have brought their construction to a high level both technically and aesthetically.

Another type of structure is the **space frame.** This is basically a kind of steel truss joined with other trusses to form a large roof. The roof needs support at only a few points along the edges. McCormick Place in Chicago is a good example.

For thousands of years shelters have been built with many different materials and structural methods, some of them strange to Western concepts. The nomads, for instance, still live in tents, which are large, comfortable and movable. The streamlined motor homes of today are just more sophisticated shelters for twentieth century nomads.

BASIC WESTERN STYLES OF ARCHITECTURE

The **Egyptians'** most important buildings were tombs. The pyramids at Giza (near Cairo) are the most well-known tombs. The other important Egyptian buildings were temples. Usually they had a tall gate and a roofed courtyard beyond, with a double row of columns. Beyond the courtyard was a hall. The Egyptians combined round columns and corniced lintels. This undoubtedly influenced the architecture of the Greeks.

Mesopotamians developed their own building style. They lived in the area between the Tigris and Euphrates Rivers in what is now Iraq. The city of ancient Babylon was located here, with great palaces and temples. These were built of soft brick which deteriorated in time. Enough is left at Persepolis to indicate the great scale and beauty of the buildings.

The ancient **Greeks** developed one of the most influential architectural styles. They reached a peak of beauty in the fifth century B.C., when they built the Parthenon on the Acropolis in Athens. This temple has sturdy columns, simple capitals, a low gable roof and refined proportions. In the Western hemisphere it has been imitated with variations many thousands of times in banks, courthouses and government buildings. There are probably more Greek temples in Washington, D.C., than there are in Athens.

The **Romans** absorbed all the best in Greek architecture, then went on to build solid and lasting structures that are most notable for their scale. The Roman Colosseum, for example, is sixteen stories high and covers an area of 300,000 square feet. The Roman buildings were more impressive than the Greek temples, but not

McCormick Place, Chicago. The space frame is a method of construction similar to a truss bridge but much more complex. Slim lengths of metal or wood are fastened together to form a light, rigid three-dimensional unit. Usually used as a roof support, it can be widely cantilevered as in the overhang shown here, which projects without any supports immediately below it.

Egyptian architecture: Temple at Luxor, *Thebes. 19th dynasty. Photograph by Elizabeth Stein.*

Greek architecture: The Parthenon, *Athens. 447-432 B.C.*

Roman architecture: Pont du Gard, *Nimes. About 1 A.D.*

Roman architecture: Maison Carrée, *Nimes. 1st century B.C. Photograph by David Barford.*

as lovely. One of the finest and best preserved Roman temples is the Maison Carrée in Nimes, France. It is set on a pedestal base which raises it half a story above the ground and allows for an impressive entrance stairway.

The chief architectural invention of the **Early Christian** builders was the basilica. This is a rectangular building with an entrance room, a long nave, and two aisles on each side, although some had only one aisle on each side. A typical basilica and a well-preserved one is Sant' Appollinare in Classe outside of Ravenna, Italy.

Early Christian architecture: St. Vitale, Ravenna. 6th century. *St. Vitale in Ravenna was built in the Early Christian era (547 A.D.), but is Byzantine in style. The walls are laid up with thin bricks with wide mortar joints. The plan is octagonal, with eight large windows in the upper story which provide light for the striking mosaics inside.*

In the sixth century A.D., while the basilica of Sant' Appollinare was under construction, an even larger and more important church was being built in Constantinople: Hagia Sophia, the Church of the Holy Wisdom. It is an outstanding example of **Early Byzantine** architecture, and one of the most spectacular buildings in the world. To stand in the center of the floor of Hagia Sophia, with the top of the huge dome eighteen stories above, gives one a feeling of space greater even than in St. Peter's in Rome.

Byzantine architecture developed small churches. These were usually in the form of a Greek cross. Four barrel-vaulted wings extended from the center square, above which rose a small dome. There are many small Byzantine churches in the old quarter of Athens. The Basilica of St. Mark's in Venice is one of the largest and best-known Byzantine churches in the West.

Early Christian architecture: Sant' Apollinare *in Classe. 6th century. Plain on the outside, the interior is a feast of light and color, of shimmering mosaics and precious inlays of marble. An arcade on each side, resting on twelve columns of veined marble, supports the triforium space below the clerestory windows.*

In southern Europe, the **Romanesque** style evolved as Roman Catholic churches and monasteries were built after the year 1000 in southern France and northern Italy. Romanesque buildings frequently have round arches and engaged columns. Nearly all Romanesque churches had towers. Ceilings were barrel vaults, and windows and doors had variations of the round arch. Romanesque designers also used wheel windows and blind arcades. One of the great Romanesque churches with its freestanding, leaning tower is at Pisa. Other fine examples are at Vezelay, Autun and Moissac.

Byzantine architecture: Ossios Lukos Monastery, *Greece.*

Byzantine architecture: St. Mark's Basilica, *Venice. Completed 1094.*

Romanesque architecture: Cathedral, Pisa, Italy. 11th century.

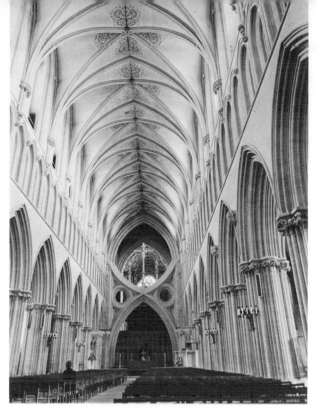

English Gothic: St. Andrews, *Wells, England. Begun 1185.*

Renaissance architecture: Santa Maria del Fiore, Florence. Begun 1435. The dome, by Brunelleschi, is the outstanding feature of the cathedral of Florence. It serves as a landmark for the entire city. The dome's octagonal main ribs spring from a high drum, and span 150 feet. With the lantern it reaches a height of 35 stories.

The **Gothic** style grew out of the Romanesque. Gothic engineers were brilliant. They had no math to speak of but plenty of experience, and they built with small stones to form tall, lightweight structures. The pointed Gothic arch gave a lighter downward thrust than the round Romanesque arch. The thin Gothic walls with their huge windows were stiffened with a splendid engineering device, the flying buttress. Thus Gothic cathedrals could have roofs that are thirty stories high and towers thirty-seven stories high, as at Amiens in France. Gothic cathedrals of great beauty were built all over Europe.

While Gothic was in its last stage of High Gothic, **Renaissance** architecture developed. It was in many ways a return to classic styles such as Greek columns and Roman arches. One of the most daring Renaissance structures is the dome designed by Filippo Brunelleschi for the church of Santa Maria del Fiore in Florence. The octagonal dome was added over the crossing many years after the church was completed.

In Rome Pope Julius II commissioned Donato Bramante in 1505 to make plans for a new St. Peters. The work went on under a succession of architects until in 1545 Pope Paul III appointed Michelangelo chief architect. Michelangelo worked on it until his death in 1564. It was finished one hundred years later when Bernini added his colonnades.

High Renaissance architecture: St. Peter's, Rome. Facade by Maderna, completed 1626.

Renaissance architecture: Church of Santo Spirito, Florence. Brunelleschi. Begun 1436. Here Brunelleschi returns architecturally to the forms of the ancient Christian basilicas, striving toward their stately simplicity.

The beginning of the sixteenth century saw a revolt, or at least a turning away, from the classical symmetry of the Renaissance toward an art of tension, of imbalance. This style is called **Mannerism,** which was first used as a negative term. The architect most often included as a Mannerist (he would have been surprised at the word) is the great Andrea Palladio of Vicenza, Italy. One of his famous buildings is the Church of San Giorgio Maggiore in Venice. The simple interior is remarkable for its austere beauty and noble proportions.

Architecture of Mannerism: Church of St. Giorgio Maggiore, Venice. Begun by Andrea Palladio, 1566. The church with its campanile and auxiliary buildings is built on an island, which serves as a landmark in the water at the end of the Grand Canal.

With the beginning of the seventeenth century, the Baroque architectural style came into being. Baroque architecture was emotional. It was fluid and organic; it was theater; but it was also orderly and precise. The open arms of Bernini's double colonnade form a welcome to St. Peter's, and his striking baldochino, the canopy over the altar, rises ten stories above St. Peter's high altar.

Early in the eighteenth century, beginning in France, the Baroque style gave way to a more fragile, curvilinear, and sophisticated style called **Rococo.** As expressed in architecture, Rococo was generally lighter and brighter than Baroque, with many forms being asymmetrical rather than in perfect balance, and with much use of mirrors and gold leaf in interiors. Decoration was rampant, in furniture and fittings as well as on walls and ceilings. The best of Rococo buildings have great charm: the Church of the Fourteen Saints in Germany, for instance, designed by Balthasar Neumann. Die Wies and Steinhausen are two splendid Rococo churches in Bavaria, designed by Dominikus Zimmerman.

Rococo architecture: Church of Die Wies, Germany. Dominikus Zimmerman, 1733.

Neo-Baroque architecture: Paris Opera House. Charles Garnier. Nearly every known decorative device has been used on the facade of Charles Garnier's Paris Opera House.

The interior is lavishly decorated, and a monumental staircase ascends to the second floor.

In the early years of the nineteenth century came a return to pseudo-classical styles, in Neo-Greek and Neo-Roman. The British Museum is an example, with its Ionic order. At the same time, Neo-Baroque buildings were constructed, a good example being the Paris Opéra. This building by Charles Garnier has a flamboyant facade with paired Greek columns and elaborate sculpture groupings.

Thus for nearly five thousand years there existed many different architectural styles. These all led up to the buildings which today are called **Modern.** Many Modern designs now have also established their place in history.

Modern architecture has been influenced by many of these preceding styles, and by modern developments in materials. Technological changes and recent world history have affected Modern architecture, too. One of the most explosive changes, though, has been the blossoming of individual freedom in design. Thus the architects themselves are sometimes the key to understanding Modern architecture.

2

MODERN MATERIALS

Throughout the nineteenth century and well into the twentieth, the preference for traditional architectural styles prevailed. Architects chose between Greek and Roman, and some went as far back as Egyptian. Others chose Baroque, Rococo or Neo-Classical, and many used a mixture of styles.

The engineers of the nineteenth century paved the way for modern architecture. Their main interest was in construction, not ostentation or ornamentation. American, British and French engineers used iron and glass in daring and imaginative ways. They flooded building interiors with light. They used iron in new ways, to support vaulted roofs with slender, delicate piers. These were economically and aesthetically superior to heavy masonry columns. The iron structures of the nineteenth century led the way for the steel skeletons now used in all large buildings.

IRON AND STEEL

Preceding the great iron buildings of the nineteenth century was a remarkable series of iron bridges. The first cast iron bridge in the world was built in Shropshire, England, by Abraham Darby. The iron bridge was built in 1779 over the River Severn. It was based on a sketch by architect Thomas Pritchard. Darby's great skill and experience enabled him to cast the ten main ribs in one piece, each of which was seventy feet long. Ironbridge, having no precedent, was based on timber construction. Some parts of the bridge are slotted to receive the other parts. The inner parts are then held in place with iron wedges.

The next important iron bridge was built in Bangor, Wales, in 1826. This suspension bridge crossing the Menai Straits was designed by Thomas Telford. It was

Iron Bridge, *Shropshire, England, 1779. Pritchard and Darby. Today the Iron Bridge appears both strong and delicate. Although restricted to pedestrian traffic now, it has withstood heavy floods and other natural forces for over two hundred years.*

Menai Bridge *over Menai Straits, Bangor, Wales, 1826. Thomas Telford.*

Bibliotheque Nationale, *Paris, 1868. Henri Labrouste.*

Clifton Bridge, *near Bristol, England, completed 1864. Isambard Kingdom Brunel.*

the world's longest suspension bridge at the time it was built, a span between towers of 579 feet. The single span of Telford's bridge is carried not by cables, which had yet to be invented, but by two huge iron chains on each side. Reminiscent of bicycle chains, these suspension members were the predecessors of the wire ropes used in contemporary suspension bridges.

One of the most talented British engineers of the nineteenth century was Isambard Kingdom Brunel. At sixteen he went to work in London with his father, Marc Brunel, who was a skilled engineer. Together the Brunels began an ambitious project, a tunnel under the Thames. Due to breaks and flooding the tunnel took nineteen years to complete. Today the East London Subway line runs through it.

At twenty-four, Isambard Brunel won a competition for a chain bridge at Clifton near Bristol, England. Although not completed until 1864, after his death, the Clifton

Forth Rail Bridge, *Queensferry, Scotland, 1890. Fowler and Baker. Photograph courtesy British Rail.*

Bridge is one of his finest works, and one of the most elegant bridges in the world. The towers are bold and simple, serving their function superbly. The principal beams are three feet deep and are suspended from triple chains on each side. The pedestrian walkways are cantilevered outboard of the beams. The Clifton Bridge is still in use every day.

One of the supreme engineering achievements of Victorian engineers in Britain is the Forth Railway Bridge at Queensferry, north of Edinburgh. The Forth Bridge is of cantilever construction, with a main span of seventeen hundred feet.

Benjamin Baker and John Fowler were the principal engineers of the Forth Bridge, completed in 1890. In place of cast and wrought iron of earlier bridges, mild steel was used to build Forth Rail Bridge. The bridge is over a mile long and more than thirty stories high, dwarfing the tiny-looking trains that cross it.

A pioneer American bridge builder was James Eads. During the Civil War he designed iron-clad river boats for the Union cause, and when the war ended he began to design a bridge across the Mississippi at St. Louis. He was appointed chief engineer when the bridge project was approved, and after eight years the bridge was completed and formally opened by President U.S. Grant on July 4, 1874.

The Eads Bridge is a monumental structure, the first ever to make extensive use of steel, the first with tubular ribs and the first built entirely by cantilever construction.

Two years after Eads began his bridge in St. Louis, John Roebling's Brooklyn Bridge was started in New York City. Roebling became well-known in America as a designer of suspension bridges. His world-famous Brooklyn Bridge was conceived in 1857 but not begun until twelve years later.

Eads Bridge, *St. Louis, Missouri, 1874*. James Eads. *The Eads Railway Bridge over the Mississippi at St. Louis rests on stone piers and was the first to use tubular-framed arches. Its cantilever construction is unusual, achieved without supports below. Every part of its three 500-foot spans can be easily removed and replaced.*

Brooklyn Bridge, *New York City, 1883*. John and Washington Roebling. *Great piers of granite, strong in compression, join with steel wires, strong in tension, to form one of the world's finest bridges.*

Maria Pia Bridge, *Oporto, Portugal, 1877. Gustave Eiffel. This graceful span crossing the Douro River in Oporto, Portugal is one of many of Gustave Eiffel's delicately designed railway bridges that preceded his famous tower in Paris.*

Just as work on the bridge was about to begin, John Roebling died from tetanus poisoning incurred in an accident while examining the bridge site. It fell to his son, Washington Roebling, to complete the bridge from his father's plans. President Chester Arthur formally opened the bridge on May 24, 1883.

Standing bold and majestic across the East River, the Brooklyn Bridge is a superb monument to the skill and ingenuity of John Roebling. The granite towers are strong and functional and offer bold contrasts to the gossamer threads of the vertical suspender cables and diagonal storm stays. Part of the strong visual impression of the bridge is due to the vigorous curve of the roadway.

France's great bridge-builder of the nineteenth century was Gustave Eiffel. He is best known for his famous tower in Paris, yet Eiffel designed and constructed many outstanding bridges in France and Portugal. His use of open webbing in piers and beams prevented the wind from damaging the more than fifty bridges constructed by Eiffel and Company.

Two of Eiffel's most spectacular bridges are the Maria Pia Bridge at Oporto, Portugal, and the Garabit Viaduct in central France. The Maria Pia Bridge over the Douro River was completed in 1877. It is a lace-like structure of parabolic arches with a light trusswork roadway. Its two main piers rest on stone platforms, and two more sets of piers support the roadway.

IRON AND GLASS

Early in the nineteenth century cast iron emerged as an important building material. Its importance was due to four factors. It was cheap. It was much more fire-resistant than wood. It would support heavy loads. And it was fairly easy to manufacture.

An open framework of cast iron and glass made it possible to create light-filled spaces of considerable size. Often these had considerable charm, as well.

One of the earliest uses of cast iron in building was made by John Nash. Nash was a well-known architect who had transformed whole streets in London.

In 1815 the English Prince George commissioned him to begin work on the Royal Pavilion in Brighton. Nash built upon a small existing pavilion and extended it to

Royal Pavilion, *Brighton, England, 1818. John Nash. This fantastic Indian style creation, with its large onion dome over the main section, was built for Prince Regent George. The bulbous cupola was built over a cast iron framework, and many of the exterior decorative elements are of cast iron as well. These cast iron structural members were thin and delicate compared to heavier construction in timber and stone.*

make the present building, topped with onion domes and minarets. The main cupola was built over a cast iron framework. The interior columns are tall slender piers of cast iron. Those in the kitchen are topped with palm leaves in metal, a somewhat overwrought suggestion of live palm trees—royal palms, at that.

The Palm House at Kew Gardens, near London, is another fine use of iron and glass. Except for the top galleries and entrance vaults, all exterior surfaces are curved. The frames are slender and the mullions very thin, so the building was a success—light and airy with a glass roof supported by light wooden beams, which in turn rested on slender iron columns. The Palm House was designed by Richard Turner and planned by Decimus Burton. It was begun in 1844.

Interior, Royal Pavilion. *John Nash personally designed the ironwork and carpentry that supports the ceilings in many rooms of the Royal Pavilion. The capitals of the columns in the music room shown here illustrate cast iron's capabilities for delicate fantasy.*

Palm House, *Kew Gardens, London, England, 1848. Decimus Burton, Richard Turner. Six stories high at the center, the Palm House in Kew Gardens is constructed entirely of iron and glass. All the roofs are curved, and inside are high balconies and spiral staircases of iron. The Palm House received more acclaim when finished than the Crystal Palace did later.*

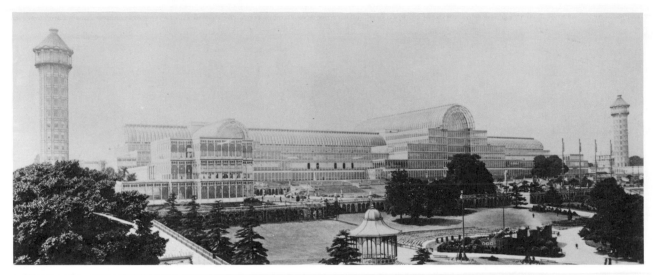

Crystal Palace, *London, England, 1851. Joseph Paxton. Photograph, National Monuments Record, London. Enormous as it was, the Crystal Palace was constructed using a simple system of small prefabricated parts. The largest sheets of glass were only four feet long. They were placed in wooden frames that rested on iron girders and were supported by cast iron pillars. This serial arrangement of small units covered eight hundred thousand square feet and was erected within six months.*

Crystal Palace, *interior. Photograph, National Monuments Record, London. The cast iron pillars supporting the vaulting of the Crystal Palace were so slender, they resembled contemporary steel scaffolding. The span of the vault was not exceptional, nor did it need to be to light the interior, since the walls themselves were largely of glass.*

The Crystal Palace, in London, represented another step in modern architecture. In 1849 an international design competition was held for a building to house a manufactured goods exhibition. All 245 entries were rejected. Joseph Paxton entered late, and won. Paxton's plans called for a larger version of a successful structure he had already built. His early lily-house used the novel construction plan of radiating ribs strengthened by concentric cross pieces, similar to the strong ribs Paxton had noticed in lily leaves.

The Crystal Palace was a rectangle 1851 feet long, the number to correspond with the year it opened. Paxton, an early ecologist, decided to add a central transept high enough to accomodate the Hyde Park elms which otherwise would have been cut down. The Crystal Palace was a simple arrangement of small standardized parts. In fact, it was the first prefabricated building. This giant structure was actually moved from Hyde Park several miles south to Sydenham, where it burned down in 1936.

Some critics did not like the building. John Ruskin, for example, called it a cucumber frame. Most Londoners were delighted with it. They saw it as the first great building not of masonry construction, and recognized it as a forward step in architecture.

Paddington Station, *London, England, 1850. Isambard Kingdom Brunel. The London railraod stations were some of the largest and finest iron and glass structures of the nineteenth century. As in Paddington Station, they were built to cover huge spans, using prefabricated wrought iron ribs and cast iron pillars. The very simplicity of construction achieved an aesthetic result.*

Paddington Station, *detail. The details of Paddington's iron work appear merely decorative at first, but they are structurally functional. The petal-forms on the ribs serve to reinforce them, and the built-up capitals atop the pillars serve as bases for the side beams.*

Isambard Kingdom Brunel, in addition to his skill at designing bridges, railways and ships, such as the steamship Great Eastern, was also the designer of Paddington Station, in London, and the railway station in Bristol. Brunel's Paddington Station, completed in 1854, proved that cast iron and mass-produced glass could cover a large area cheaply and effectively without requiring massive foundations. The station is a huge barrel vault covering a space for six tracks and five platforms. The decorative elements on the ribs and columns were designed by Digby Wyatt. Brunel's design for Paddington exemplifies economy, simplicity and lucidity, and is altogether satisfactory.

Two of the great French iron-and-glass buildings of the nineteenth century are the Parisian libraries, the Bibliotheque Genevieve and the Bibliotheque Nationale, both designed by architect Henri Labrouste. They were completed in 1850 and 1868, respectively. While neither building has the exterior lightness of the buildings of Burton and Paxton, the interiors show skill in the use of cast iron. The reading room of the Bibliotheque Genevieve is a great double barrel vaulted hall designed with daring and imagination.

There are two outstanding features of the Bibliotheque Nationale. One is the reading room, which has sixteen slim columns rising thirty-two feet. From their tops spring slender girders which join to form nine domes. In the center of each dome is a round skylight which illuminates the reading desks below.

The book storage area is even more impressive. The center area of this *magasin central* is four stories high, with the stacks on each side connected by bridges. The floors and stair steps all are an open gridwork of pierced iron, allowing light to penetrate through each floor.

Bibliotheque Nationale, *Paris. Study Room. The Study Room of the Bibliotheque Nationale is also of iron construction, with slim pillars in pairs supporting the capitals from which the arches spring. As in the reading room, semi-circular iron girders form the framework for the arches. Generous skylights flood the room with light.*

French engineer Jules Saulnier's best-known building was erected in the middle of the Marne River at Noisiel-sur-Marne near Paris in 1872. It was built to house the Menier Chocolate Works. Today there is a modern factory manufacturing chocolate at the same site.

Saulnier's factory has a complete iron frame carried by masonry piers built into the bed of the River Marne. Power was supplied by water wheels between the piers. The structure is virtually a bridge, with one story between the piers and four more above them. A braced iron frame carries the weight of the walls, which are light hollow brick decorated with colored ceramic tiles and laid in panels between the iron frames.

Menier Chocolate Works, *Noisiel-sur-Marne, France, 1872. Jules Saulnier.*

Some of the most interesting and engaging examples of iron-and-glass architecture of the nineteenth century are glass-covered passages reserved for pedestrians. In Paris there are more than a dozen of these galleries still in use. They are clean, neat and well-maintained, and range in age from the Passage du Caire of 1799 to the Galerie Vivienne of 1828 which is one of the most impressive.

A fitting end to this section on nineteenth century iron structures is a mention of Gustave Eiffel's thousand-foot tower for the Paris Universal Exposition of 1889. Of all modern structures described in this book, the Eiffel Tower is probably the best known. Eiffel's background as a designer of bridges over wind-swept valleys had prepared him for this construction.

Galerie Vivienne, *Paris, 1828. In the area of Paris between the Boulevard Montmartre and the Palais Royal are a half dozen galleries or "passages." More than covered shopping streets, they include workshops, offices and living quarters. These galleries are the forerunners of the modern shopping malls—many shops under one roof, the pedestrian shopper protected from the weather.*

Galleria Vittorio Emanuele II, *Milan, Italy, 1867. Guiseppe Mengoni. One of the largest and finest galleries in the world, the Galleria Vittorio Emanuele stretches a thousand feet and its octagonal dome is almost as big as St. Peter's. Contemporary architects Philip Johnson, I.M. Pei, Gyo Obata and others have used the gallery concept for large open areas several hundred feet long, calling them "gallerias."*

Eiffel Tower, *Paris, 1889. Gustave Eiffel.*

The best way to experience the Tower is to get inside it, by walking up or down the fifty stories between the ground and the first platform. Then all the strength, all the boldness, all the scope of Eiffel's constructive genius can be seen and appreciated at first hand. This splendid monument has become the symbol of Paris, despite the fact that many French architects and writers petitioned that it never be built.

The best way to see the Eiffel Tower is to walk down through it, even if that is a descent of fifty-two stories. Looking up through the four giant legs, they seem almost transparent.

REINFORCED CONCRETE

Toward the end of the nineteenth century the preference for iron and steel as building materials began to give way to reinforced concrete. Concrete alone had been in use since Roman times. It was useful in walls and columns, which are under compression, but no good in beams, which are under tension as well.

In 1868 French gardener Joseph Monier began to embed a wire mesh in concrete, in the manufacture of tubs and tanks. Today, reinforced concrete consists of steel rods embedded in concrete. Concrete is a mixture of sand, washed gravel, cement and water. In certain constructions, in parts of some Maillart bridges, for instance, there seems to be almost as much iron as concrete, but generally the proportion of iron is small.

François Hennebique, born in France in 1842, was the first architect to use reinforced concrete on a large scale. He used it for mills and silos in France, granaries in Italy and sanatoria in Switzerland. Hennebique was the first architect to build a structure as a complete reinforced frame, from foundation to roof, incorporating his own system to join beams and slabs.

One of the pioneers of reinforced concrete was Auguste Perret. One of Perret's finest buildings is his church of Notre Dame at Le Raincy, eleven miles east of Paris. Completed in 1922, Le Raincy is Perret's outstanding statement in reinforced concrete. The roof is a triple barrel vault of shallow arc. It rests on slender concrete columns. The walls are thin concrete panels, inlaid with stained glass. Several young architects worked with Perret and were indebted to him for their understanding of the potential of reinforced concrete. The best known of these was Le Corbusier, whose work is discussed later.

Eugene Freyssinet, born in 1879, was a talented engineer who made some revolutionary discoveries in the use of reinforced concrete. Freyssinet was well-trained in mathematics, yet stressed the use of intuition in arriving at design solutions.

At the age of twenty-five Freyssinet conceived the idea of "pre-stressing" concrete. Put very simply, this process consists of stretching steel wire under high tension in the middle of the concrete casting form. Then concrete is poured around the steel. When the concrete has matured, the tension of the wire is released.

Freyssinet's prestressed concrete beams allowed him to build bridges that are slim, lightweight and extremely strong. Five of these bridges were built over the River Marne near Paris. These are light, delicate spans whose I-beam webs are only four inches thick.

A fourth French architect who used reinforced concrete was Tony Garnier. Garnier, born in Lyon in 1869, was appointed city architect of Lyon when he was thirty-six. There he carried out a series of large buildings in reinforced concrete—hospitals, stockyards, abbatoirs, the city stadium. In 1934 one of his finest buildings was completed, the city hall of Boulogne-Billancourt, west of Paris.

Notre Dame du Raincy, *Raincy, France, 1922. August Perret. Perret used reinforced concrete to create this unadorned tower as the spire of his church at Le Raincy just east of Paris. Twenty years after the Rue Franklin apartments Perret had become a master of ferroconcrete construction, and this simple and graceful bell tower is a splendid example of his skill.*

Tony Garnier spent a long, full life as an architect, yet it is the visionary drawings he made as a young man in Rome that have made him famous. During his three years at the Villa Medici, as winner of the Prix de Rome, Tony Garnier developed a large series of drawings, meticulous in detail, of an imaginary city he called the Cite Industrielle. This plan for a city of 35,000 was a revolutionary concept and was recognized as such, the first comprehensive town plan of the century.

In Garnier's plans, the residential area is separated from the industrial area by a green belt. The main railway line enters the city through a subway, and arrives at a handsome terminal. Mid-city holds a civic center, the high school area and an elaborate sports complex. All the buildings were to be made of reinforced concrete.

Notre Dame du Raincy, *interior. The slender concrete columns support the curved concrete slabs of the roof of the church at Le Raincy. The prefabricated wall screens are made entirely of perforated concrete and glass, and are non-loadbearing. The slim reinforced columns support the whole structure.*

Bridge at Esbly, *France, 1946. Eugene Freyssinet. The incredible slenderness of the Esbly Bridge was made possible by Freyssinet's process of prestressing the concrete units of the structure. This long span of thin concrete seems to fly over the River Marne twenty miles east of Paris. The spare simplicity of the railing completes the elegant effect.*

City Hall, Boulogne-Billancourt, *interior. Belied by the plain exterior, the four-story interior of the city hall building shows an exciting use of cantilevered floors surrounding a large open area well lighted by clerestory windows. The uncluttered expanse of the ground floor gives a feeling of spaciousness. The plan has many similarities to Wright's Larkin Building.*

City Hall, Boulogne-Billancourt, *France. Tony Garnier. Photograph courtesy Mayor's Office, Boulogne-Billancourt. The rather plain facade of this building on the southern edge of Paris reflects its construction of reinforced concrete. This was the chosen material of architect Garnier, who had planned for its use in his dream city, his Cité Industrielle.*

3

PIONEERS IN MODERN DESIGN

Red House, Bexley Heath, Kent, England, 1860. Philip Webb. Photograph courtesy National Monuments Record, London. Built for British designer William Morris, Red House is modern in the sense that it has a freshness and originality that breaks away from Victorian tradition. The interplay of gabled roofs, the walls of brick with minimal use of stone, the round windows below the eaves combine to create a pleasing effect.

La Citta Nuova, Project, 1914. Antonio Sant' Elia. Photograph courtesy Civic Museum of Como, Italy. This is one of several careful drawings by Sant' Elia of a complex of skyscraper towers rising from a multi-level circulation of roads, railways and canals. The elements in this elegant perspective anticipate many aspects of modern buildings: provision for the movement of trains, barges and road traffic.

The development of modern building materials led to changes in construction methods. Together these allowed imaginative architects to develop new concepts of space and form. Before these blossomed into the Modern style, many individuals created unique designs. They sowed the seed for the tremendous design changes that have emerged in the past century or more.

This chapter looks at some of the structures created by the pioneers in modern design, and then looks at Art Nouveau architecture. The Art Nouveau style lasted only briefly, but it was the first unified style to appear after the sudden development of modern materials.

Philip Webb and Norman Shaw

In England, influential architects after 1850 were best known for their house designs. Two of the most important architects were Philip Webb and Norman Shaw. Both associated closely with William Morris, who was a founder of the English Arts and Crafts movement. Morris was aghast at the bad design of the current machine made objects. He felt that good design could only return in handmade works fashioned with the loving care of the artisan.

In 1860, Philip Webb built a house for William Morris at Bexley Heath, outside of London. This is perhaps his best-known house, called Red House because it is built of red brick. The furnishings were designed by both Webb and Morris. Several aspects of the house mark it as a new departure in design. The brick is exposed, not covered with stucco. The house is planned from the inside out, making the facade secondary. And the interior construction is clearly visible.

Richard Norman Shaw was a successful commercial architect. He designed many fine office buildings in London, including New Scotland Yard, but he is known best for his country houses. Leyswood House, one of the first of his large country houses, and other houses by Shaw were early influences on Frank Lloyd Wright. The massive chimneys, steep gables and large window groupings of Leywsood can be found in many of Wright's early houses in Oak Park.

Beginning in 1877 Shaw took over the design for Bedford Park. With its large gardens preserving old trees, it is a pleasant place near Kew Gardens in London. The publication of Shaw's sketches and house plans helped lead to the ''Shingle Style'' of the early eighties in America. Frank Lloyd Wright's first house in Oak Park, Illinois, was influenced by the Shingle Style.

Leyswood House, *Rotherfield, E. Sussex, England, 1869. Norman Shaw. Photograph courtesy I. Simpson.*

Charles Voysey

Charles Voysey spent his first years designing wallpapers and textiles, and then turned to designing residences. One of his best known houses is Moor Crag, which is characteristic of Voysey's earlier small houses. In Moor Crag, the volumes and surfaces of the country cottage have been rearranged into a complex and pleasing form. The walls are of stucco and the highpitched roof of slate. Windows are grouped horizontally and framed in stone; tall chimneys punctuate the roof line.

In Germany, the Expressionist architects were not primarily out to shock the public. They wanted to show that buildings could be something beyond the standard Neo-Classical pomposities. This was a radical change for architects, a revolt against traditional styles. They moved toward forms that were visionary and often fantastic and unconventional.

Many of the most provocative pieces of Expressionist architecture remain sketches, partly because the engineering abilities needed were not yet developed.

Moor Crag, *Cartmel Fell, Cumbria, England. C.F.A. Voysey. Photograph courtesy National Monuments Record, London.*

Peter Behrens

Peter Behrens, born in Hamburg in 1868, served as a bridge between more traditional architecture and the Expressionist approach. In 1909 he designed his most famous building, the AEG Turbine Factory. Here the structural elements are presented in a direct and rational manner and the window treatment is lively and functional. In his private practice he employed three of the great architects of the twentieth century—Walter Gropius, Ludwig Mies van der Rohe and Le Corbusier.

A.E.G. Turbine Factory, Berlin, Germany, 1909. Peter Behrens. Photograph courtesy Landesbildstelle, Berlin. The great Turbine Erecting Shop for the A.E.G., Germany's giant electric company, combines sloping walls of glass with massive masonry corner elements. The light steel frames of the street facade form one of the earliest curtain walls. The faceted gable roof is reminiscent of the large barns of rural Germany.

Interior, Grosses Schauspielhaus, Berlin, 1919. Hans Poelzig. Photograph courtesy Akademie der Kunste, Berlin. This, the most famous of Poelzig's works, was designed with and for theater director Max Reinhardt. The interior is perhaps the finest example of Expressionist architecture.

Hans Poelzig

Expressionist architect Hans Poelzig created a most unusual and imaginative design for a theater in Berlin, the Grosses Schauspielhaus. The huge dome of the interior of the theater is studded with myriads of stalactite pendants tipped with reflectors. These give the illusion of a fairy grotto, a mysterious cave-like atmosphere which helps prepare the theatergoer for the coming drama on the stage.

Glass Pavilion, *Cologne, 1914. Bruno Taut. Photograph courtesy Akademie der Kunste, Berlin. Nearly all of this extraordinary structure was made of glass. The diamond-shaped panels of the multi-faceted dome were of colored glass on the inside and clear plate glass on the exterior. The dome rested on a drum of glass bricks and slender concrete posts. Even the doors were of glass.*

Interior, Glass Pavilion. Photograph courtesy Akademie der Kunste, Berlin. Both inner and outer staircase walls of the Glass Pavilion were of glass blocks set into a steel framework. The steps themselves, both treads and risers, were also of glass. Taut's skillful and imaginative use of glass permitted a striking contrast of light against the black of the steel framework.

Einstein Tower, Potsdam, Germany, 1921. Erich Mendelsohn. Photograph courtesy Akademie der Kunste, Berlin. The Einstein Tower is an early and impressive example of the plastic possibilities of concrete. The outer curves of the entrance hall invite the visitor up a short flight of steps leading through a bowl-shaped space to the main staircase. The eye-like windows are indented on either side in a rhythmic ascendancy, and the monolithic structure is topped by a cupola for the observatory. There is a Gaudí-like quality to the whole concept.

A contemporary of Hans Poelzig was Bruno Taut. His most original work was his Glass Pavilion, completed for an exhibition in Cologne in 1914. The walls of Taut's building were of glass block, and even the treads and risers of the circular staircase were of glass. Inside, under the dome, was a waterfall cascading down five levels. Built for the German glass manufacturers, Taut's pavilion was, for its time, an extraordinary and imaginative combination of glass and steel, a dazzling *tour de force* not to be matched for many years.

Erich Mendelsohn

Erich Mendelsohn designed a memorable small observatory for Professor Albert Einstein. The building was completed in Potsdam in 1921. Here Mendelsohn explored the sculptural qualities inherent in reinforced concrete. The windows are set into sculptured recesses. The tower is topped by a dome.

Centenary Hall, *Breslau (Wroclaw), 1913. Max Berg, architect; Trauer, engineer. Photograph courtesy Akademie der Kunste, Berlin. This huge domed structure was built of reinforced concrete. The radiating ribs fan out from the central compression ring and rest on a lower ring supported by massive arches. Four concentric bands of clerestory windows flood the interior with light.*

Petersdorff Department Store, *Breslau, Germany, now Wroclaw, Poland, 1927. Erich Mendelsohn. Photograph courtesy Akademie der Kunste, Berlin. The sweeping curves of the cantilevered corner depend on specially curved glass panes for their harmonious effect. Mendelsohn's stores became examples for other western department stores built in later years.*

Mendelsohn also designed fine department stores for the Schocken Company, in Petersdorff, Stuttgart and Chemnitz. They are distinguished by their sophisticated window design and dynamic combinations of flat and curved forms.

Max Berg

Max Berg was not really an Expressionist in his architecture. His most famous building is the *Jahrhundert*, or Centenary, Hall, completed in Breslau in 1913. Breslau is now Wroclaw, Poland, and the Centenary Hall of Max Berg and his engineer Trauer is now the People's Palace. The exterior of the building is rather plain, but the soaring concrete ribs and the circular rows of windows inside proclaim Berg's fine understanding of the technical uses of reinforced concrete coupled with a remarkable feeling for its aesthetic possibilities. The thirty-two concrete ribs span an area of 21,000 square feet; the circular abutment ring is 213 feet in diameter. Berg's concept has a majesty and grandeur seldom found again in the twentieth century until the works of Pier Luigi Nervi.

Goldman and Salatsch Store (Loos House), *Vienna, 1911. Adolf Loos. The facade of this store in Vienna is plain and uncompromising, following the theories of its architect that ornament is wasteful and unjustified. The severe orchestration of the sixty-four punched windows is in contrast to the rich marble surfaces of the lower stories. Four modified Doric columns support a broad steel beam and above each column is a square stone pier.*

Adolf Loos

In Austria Adolf Loos was a pioneer of modern architecture. He became an outspoken critic of the ornamental excesses of Vienna's Art Nouveau architects. Loos wrote that "anyone who listens to Beethoven's Ninth then sits down to design wallpaper is either a rogue or a degenerate."

Some of Loos' most distinctive designs were for large private homes. His larger building on the Michaelerplatz in Vienna is a handsome combination of a richly-clad lower section (the store front) and a completely unadorned upper part with a simple roof line. His theories, his continual fight against traditionalism and mediocrity in architecture, and his splendid houses have earned Adolf Loos an honored place in architectural history.

Petrus Berlage

Holland's leading pioneer of modern architecture was Hendrick Petrus Berlage. His most famous building is the Amsterdam Stock Exchange, completed in 1903. In this building there are three great halls, housing the commodities, grain and stock markets. The commodities market is the most impressive, almost seventy feet wide, with a gable roof of glass and iron eight stories high at the apex. There are broad arcades in each side wall and arcaded galleries above them.

Berlage's last building was the municipal museum for the Hague, completed in 1929. The blockiness of its main forms resembles the Unity Temple, completed in 1906 in Oak Park by Frank Lloyd Wright. Berlage was influential in bringing Wright's work to the attention of Dutch architects. Berlage's own works, his ideas and his philosophy considerably influenced modern Dutch architecture.

Interior, Stock Exchange, Amsterdam, 1903. H.P. Berlage. Photograph courtesy Netherlands Embassy, Washington, D.C. The interior of the Amsterdam Stock Exchange, although remodeled in later years, demonstrates Berlage's insistence that the most important art of the architect is the creation of space. Rising from the gallery walls, broad steel girder arches support the glass roof.

Gemeente Museum, The Hague, Netherlands, 1935. H.P. Berlage. Photograph courtesy Escher Foundation, The Hague.

Antonio Sant' Elia

Antonio Sant' Elia, an Italian, is regarded as the architect of Futurism. Futurism was an Italian movement in the arts begun in 1909 by poet Filippo Marinetti. In 1910 a group of Italian painters published a manifesto of Futurism. Soon writers, sculptors, musicians and dramatists were publishing manifestos.

Futurism was a violent protest against historical styles so imbedded in Italian art and architecture. Futurist painters and architects found a new beauty in the machine, and glorified the mechanical aspects of art over traditional imitation of beauty.

Because Sant' Elia died young, killed in action in World War I, he was never able to complete one building. Even so, he is known internationally for an extraordinary series of drawings he created. These were his design for an imaginary city which he called the *Città Nuova*, or New City. These exceptionally handsome drawings have been published and well distributed and give him his place in architectural history.

In July of 1914 Sant' Elia published the Futurist Manifesto of Architecture. He said, "It is time to be done with funereal decorative architecture; architecture must be something more vital than that; we can best attain that something by blowing sky-high, for a start, all those monuments and monumental pavements, arcades, and flights of steps." And, "We no longer feel ourselves to be men of the cathedrals and ancient town halls, but men of the Grand Hotels, railway stations, giant roads, colossal harbors, covered markets, and glittering arcades."

4

ART NOUVEAU ARCHITECTURE

Art Nouveau was essentially a European movement spanning the two decades between 1890 and 1910. In this period, many painters, sculptors, designers and architects abandoned traditional styles based on the historicism of the nineteenth century. They began expressing their own inventiveness and individualism through designs rich in swirling, graceful curves.

Victor Horta 1861–1947

Victor Horta was the first architect to produce an Art Nouveau building. This was the Tassel House built in Brussels in 1893. The exterior of the Tassel House is smooth stone. The most impressive feature is a large two-story-high bay window, supported by a curved iron beam at the bottom. Another curved iron beam supports a balcony above the windows. The columns in between have distinctively Art Nouveau styling. The building's interior is sumptuously decorated. A sinuous iron staircase sweeps upward, and the wall of the stairway is covered with exuberant ornament.

Following the Tassel House, Horta designed a residence for the celebrated chemist Ernest Solvay. This building was completed in 1895 in Brussels. The walls of the Solvay House curve forward to frame a recessed center area. This has an elegant ironwork balcony above the ground floor. The interior of the Solvay House is especially rich and harmonious, and the street and garden doors are fine examples of Horta's Art Nouveau arabesques in iron.

Tassel House, Brussels, 1893. Victor Horta. This house represents the beginning of Art Nouveau in architecture. The ordinary family house is here transformed into a rhythmic and harmonious composition which fits well between its neighbors.

Gate House, Guell Park, Barcelona, 1900-1914. Antonio Gaudi. The roof of one of two gate houses for Guell Park is covered with small broken ceramic tiles conforming to the sculptural surfaces. The perforated pinnacle is a chimney pot.

Entrance to Solvay House, Brussels, 1874. Victor Horta. This one entrance illustrates Horta's skill in designing for wood, stone and metal. Rich ironwork patterns grace the railing of the balcony and the grillwork behind the windows of the carved wooden door. But more striking is the carving on the outside of the stone consoles or brackets supporting the balcony. Here the subtle reversing of the inner curve is true sculpture.

Delhaye House, 1898 (left), and van Eetvelde House, 1895, Brussels. Victor Horta. These two town houses on Avenue Palmerston reveal a considerable change in Horta's approach. Delhaye, on the corner, is completely asymmetric, with many different window shapes and styles. On the side street is an unusual triangular bay. Each of the six front windows varies in size and design. The earlier van Eetvelde house has an almost rigidly symmetric facade.

Entrance Door, Delhaye House. Even with its mottled stonework the Delhaye entrance door has charm. On the door window Horta's whiplash grillwork is again evident. The helmeted stone pillars flanking the doorway have over-tones of both Gaudí and Guimard. A nice touch is the footscraper at lower right.

Door Handle, Horta House, Brussels, 1898. Victor Horta. The interior of Horta's own house, which is now a museum, is richly appointed and has much of the furniture built in. Everything was designed by Horta, even the door handles.

Hector Guimard 1867–1942

Hector Guimard began his career in 1888, searching for a new style. After travels to England and to Belgium, where he met and talked with Victor Horta, he returned to Paris to complete his plans for Castel Béranger, the first building to incorporate his concepts of Art Nouveau. Castel Béranger is a large apartment house on rue La Fontaine. Its exterior is largely Neo-Gothic, but the interior and the decoration are Art Nouveau.

Guimard wanted to plan and supervise construction of every detail of his buildings, from entrance gate to doorknobs. To do this, he began to learn fabrication techniques for many materials. He studied their design possibilities. In the iron foundry, for instance, he saw that he could give dynamic form to the stem shapes which he planned for the Métro entrances, to avoid using iron in a dull, static way.

The system of subway entrances which Guimard designed for the Paris Métro system in 1900 brought his art to the attention of nearly every citizen in Paris, most of whom had never seen his buildings. Altogether one hundred forty of Guimard's Métro entrances were installed. More than ninety of them still survive. All the components were cast in modular, exchangeable units, so the Métro entrances were an early example of successful prefabrication. The two main parts of each entrance are the railings and the archways. The railings have two patterns, abstract curvilinear forms cast in iron. The archways are two "stalks" of cast iron that seem to grow out of the low stone parapets at the curb. These stalks end above in specially-cast bud-shaped light shades made of amber glass. Branching from each side stalk to the center are bars holding the Métro's sign.

Entrance Door, Castel Béranger, Paris, 1895. Hector Guimard. *This wrought iron and copper entrance door is the most art nouveau expression in Guimard's Castel Béranger. Highly original carved stone columns make a frame for the whiplash curves and powerful forms of the door. The wrought iron elements vary in width from pencil-thin to several inches thick.*

Métro Entrance, Porte Dauphine, Paris, 1900. Hector Guimard. The only complete fanlight Guimard Métro entrance left in Paris is now protected as a historical monument. An iron-and-glass skylight beyond the fanlight protects the pedestrians from the weather. Porcelain enameled panels in orange line the inner walls.

Detail, Métro Entrance, Porte Dauphine. An excellent example of Guimard's use of the stem of a plant for design inspiration. He agreed with Horta that the stem of a plant was the more useful design element. The ironwork has been painted green, part of which has eroded, giving a pleasant patina and a suggestion of vegetation.

Guimard House, *Paris, 1909. Hector Guimard.*

One of Guimard's fine residential designs is that of his own house on Avenue Mozart in Paris. The Guimard House is triangular, on a narrow corner lot. The windows of the two street facades offer almost too much variety. The exterior would have been more unified without the protruding dormer windows on the roof. Inside, the living and dining rooms are elliptical. They fit well into the triangular floor plan. Guimard designed all the furniture, fittings, wall modeling and chandeliers.

By 1911 Guimard's facades had become symmetrical, as in the rue Pavée synagogue. This has an undulating facade of stone, with eighteen tall, narrow windows in the center, grouped in rows of six. The principal carved decoration is over the three windows above the entrance doors. The interior is long and narrow, and five stories high, lighted by a huge window at the back and by large skylights.

One of the best of Guimard's last works in Paris is the apartment building at 18 rue Henri Heine, completed in 1926. Guimard and his wife made their last home in Paris in a third floor flat in these apartments. When he was seventy-one, in 1938, Guimard and his wife left for New York. There he died, almost unknown, four years later.

Interior of synagogue, Rue Pavee, Paris, 1913. Hector Guimard. The synagogue in the fourth arrondisement is a tall, narrow building rather plain on the outside but richly colored and decorated on the interior. The skylight and great window to the west are sparingly ornamented, but the columns, capitals and balcony rails are liberally decorated. A Guimard fantasy is the bud-like shape of the light bulbs.

Otto Wagner 1841–1918

Otto Wagner was the most notable Austrian architect of the Art Nouveau movement. For his family he designed the first Villa Wagner, completed in 1886. It is rather pretentious, an Italianate palazzo design with scarcely a square yard of undecorated surface. On the front, double diagonal staircases lead to a covered porch. The porch roof is supported by four twenty-foot-high columns topped by gilded Ionic capitals. The porch ceiling is gilded and painted, as are the iron brackets which support it. On the left was another large open porch. This is now enclosed by a luminous mural in stained glass.

Villa Wagner I, Vienna, 1886. Otto Wagner. The pretentious exterior of this country house by and for Wagner was designed when he had built very few buildings. A mixture of neoclassic and neobaroque, it nevertheless has a stately symmetry. The sculptured figure was added by a later owner.

Karlsplatz Station, *Vienna, 1899. Otto Wagner.*

In 1894, Wagner was commissioned to design the stations and some of the bridges for Vienna's elevated transport system, the Stadtbahn. The most interesting of his Stadtbahn stations is the one at Karlsplatz, completed in 1898. The two small buildings for this station are closer to Art Nouveau style than Wagner's earlier works. The central part of each is roofed with a barrel vault. Romanesque arches curve over the doorways. Extending on each side are small rooms lighted by porthole windows. The outer walls consist of two rows of white-painted metal panels set in thin iron frames. Much of the exterior surface is decorated with gold-leafed stencil patterns.

Other Wagner buildings of 1898 are two apartment houses on the Linke Wienzeile, numbers 38 and 40. Number 38 is a five-story apartment building with shops on the ground floor. The facade is of white stucco, plain on the two lower floors but embellished with gold-leafed medallions and trailing leaf-forms on the upper stories.

Number 40, next door, is called the "Majolica House" because its flat facade is covered with a distinctive Art Nouveau pattern in colored ceramic tile. The ceramic colors are primarily pink, green and gray. This may seem an unlikely combination, yet because they are soft and subdued, it works. Wagner has solved the problem of joining the Majolica House unobtrusively to its contiguous neighbors by adding a vertical row of recessed balconies on each side, using deep green tiles on the wall surfaces. Both apartment houses are still in use and in good repair.

"Majolica House," Link Wienzeile No. 40, *Vienna, 1899. Otto Wagner. The facade of Link Wienzeile No. 40 is completely flat, except for some ornaments at the top. The red and green floral decoration in ceramic tile covering the front gave the Majolica House its nickname. Iron floral patterns on the balcony railings match those of the facade.*

The best known of Wagner's buildings, and one still in use, is the Post Office Savings Bank, completed in Vienna in 1906. The facade is off-white marble slabs attached by massive aluminum bolts. Its upper section is elaborate, adorned with sculpture by Othmar Shimkowitz. The interior of the bank is more distinctive. The entire ceiling of the central section is a flattened arch of frosted glass, protected by a glass roof above it. The large open room of the counter area thus has ample natural light. This ambience is more pleasing than the doubtful richness of some of today's banks.

While the Savings Bank was being constructed, Wagner was building St. Leopold's Church on the grounds of the Austrian State Hospital in Steinhof on the western edge of Vienna. St. Leopold's has Byzantine overtones but resembles the Savings Bank in several ways. The church, too, is sheathed in white marble panels. The exterior bronze sculpture is again by Shimkowitz. The flat canopy over the entrance is supported by slender aluminum poles, as in the Savings Bank.

Wagner's last completed building was his own house, the second Villa Wagner. This is smaller and simpler, more sober than the first Villa Wagner, although one misses its exuberance. Otto Wagner had a long and fruitful career during which he was given many honors, and not only in his native Austria. He was made an honorary member of the chief architectural organizations of the United States, Great Britain and the leading countries of Europe.

Post Office Savings Bank, *Vienna, 1906. Otto Wagner. This large open space in one of Wagner's finest buildings is vaulted with iron and glass. Slim flat steel posts continue above the ceiling, supporting the skylight. This simple and ingenious use of glass marks Wagner as one of the foremost architects of his time.*

St. Leopold's Church, *Am Steinhof, Vienna, 1907. Otto Wagner. Austrian Art Nouveau, as exemplified in Wagner's church Am Steinhof, is far removed from the curvilinear arabesques of Guimard and Horta. There is a stiffness and self-consciousness about the exterior ornament and the somewhat grandiose statuary that belies the charm of the interior. The church is covered with thin marble panels held in place by aluminum bolts, the same exterior sheathing as on the Post Office Savings Bank.*

Villa Wagner II, *Vienna, 1913. Otto Wagner. A strong contrast exists between this second house and last work by Wagner and the first Villa Wagner next door. Here the emphasis is on a simple flat facade having indented windows with simple frames. Restrained decoration is provided between the lower windows and on the door itself. A small stained glass window is set above the door frame.*

Joseph Olbrich 1867–1908

Joseph Maria Olbrich was one of Otto Wagner's most talented students. In 1898, he constructed one of his finest buildings, the Secession Museum in Vienna. Fifteen steps lead up to the Museum's recessed central entrance. It has plain, windowless blocks on each side and a tower base above. The stone base has short, chunky piers at each corner. Fitted between the piers is a large openwork dome of lightly-gilded metal leaf-forms. The roof rests on only six supports, leaving the interior completely free of fixed partitions. Rooms can thus be shaped to suit different exhibits.

Olbrich designed many other fine buildings, but his career was cut short by a fatal illness at forty-one. He had completed forty buildings and left behind more than 25,000 drawings.

Joseph Hoffman 1870–1956

Another fine student of Otto Wagner's was Joseph Hoffman. His first large commission was for the Purkersdorf Sanatarium, completed in 1905. This is a five-story building with a long central loggia on the third floor which divides the front evenly. Frank Lloyd Wright used much the same bilateral division four years later in his Mason City Bank, and Walter Gropius used it in his Werkbund Building of 1914.

In Hoffmann's later work, his tendency was toward the geometric, toward angular corners and white walls with black accents. A fine example of his later style is the Palais Stoclet in Brussels. Designed for a wealthy industrialist, this building is truly palatial in its size and luxurious appointments. Above the two-story living room is a gallery supported by pillars sheathed in onyx. In the dining room are murals in mosaic by Hoffmann's friend, the painter Gustave Klimt.

There are a few curves in some windows and a half-dome roof over a five-sided bay. Otherwise the exterior is rigidly rectilinear. It was once striking in its contrast of white marble panels edged by black corner and cornice strips. The effect is less impressive today, since exhaust gases and time have turned the marble gray.

Secession Gallery, *Vienna, 1898. Joseph Olbrich. This strongly symmetrical gallery is crowned by a cupola of gilded metal woven in foliage form; the Viennese called it "the golden cabbage." Except for a decorative frieze along the top and corners, the facade is completely plain.*

Palais Stoclet, *Brussels, 1905. Josef Hoffman. This is Hoffman's most notable building. The severely cubist masses are relieved by occasional arches and half-domes, but the basic approach is precise and geometric. The Palais Stoclet is closer to Art Deco than to Art Nouveau. The building is sheathed in white marble, and the corners and copings are of narrow bronze trim. Circling the prismatic tower are four sculptured athletes.*

Henry van de Velde 1863–1957

Henry van de Velde was a many-talented Belgian. He was a painter, designer, theorist and interpreter of Art Nouveau. Although not a trained architect, in 1894 he designed his own home, Bloemenwerf, as a kind of artistic manifesto. He acted as architect and designed nearly everything else: the fittings, the furniture, even his wife's clothes.

The front of Bloemenwerf is divided into three similar areas, each topped with a gambrel or double-angled gable. The exterior is cream colored stucco. The window frames and shutters are painted black. A low trapezoidal roof overhangs the doorway. Bloemenwerf is interesting as the expression of an artist, but not great architecture.

In 1902 van de Velde was invited to Weimar, Germany, by the Grand Duke of Saxe-Weimar. His mission was to build a school of applied arts and to help the local industries improve their design standards. The School of Applied Arts opened in 1908, with van de Velde as director. His revolutionary teaching methods paved the way for those used by Gropius in founding the Bauhaus ten years later. (See next chapter.) Van de Velde also designed his own house and many other houses in Germany and Holland.

Bloemenwerf House, Brussels, 1895. Henry van de Velde. Not formally trained as an architect, Belgian designer Henry van de Velde built this house for himself in a suburb of Brussels. The most cottage-like of all art nouveau houses, it combines functional structural necessities with many opportunities for decoration within. The large window above the entrance porch gave light to van de Velde's studio.

Charles Rennie Mackintosh 1868–1928

Charles Rennie Mackintosh was Scotland's Art Nouveau architect. In 1896 he won the competition for a new building for his old school, the Glasgow School of Art. Funds were limited, so the school governors asked the competing architects to design a plain building. This is what Mackintosh gave them. The School of Art is his masterpiece, a large building on a hill in Glasgow. The front of the building faces north, providing the traditional best light for the two-story high painting studios. The studio windows are exceptionally large. For a building of 1899, the window arrangement is remarkably "modern." The facade is of smooth stone, quite plain. The only exterior touches of ornament are in the carving around the north and west doors, and in the window brackets on the north.

Glasgow School of Art, Glasgow, Scotland, 1899 and 1909. Charles Rennie Mackintosh. Photograph courtesy Glasgow School of Art. Mackintosh's most important work, the Glasgow School of Art is a mixture of symmetry and non-symmetry. Rising atop a hill like a Scottish baronial castle, the facade nevertheless is most modern in the size and placement of the enormous studio windows. The impressive entranceway is off-center to the left. The lower studio window frames are buttressed by decorative wrought iron braces.

The school's most distinctive interior space is the library, completed in 1908. It is two stories high, lighted by two-story windows on the west. Framed in plain wooden posts and beams, the only carving is on a few balcony posts. A gallery around the upper perimeter gives added space.

Library, Glasgow School of Art. Photograph courtesy Glasgow School of Art. An open gallery encircles the upper part of the library, a large room seventeen feet high. Two rows of columns support the gallery and continue upward to support the ceiling. The gallery beams are extended outward to join the columns, an unusual and effective structural device. Large windows light both upper and lower floors.

Lower floor of Library, Glasgow School of Art. Photograph courtesy Glasgow School of Art. Mackintosh's way of using his beam-and-column timber framework in the library is reminiscent of Japanese structural methods. The posts form a kind of open partition separating the periodicals desk from the study tables. Light is brought in by clerestory windows in the upper story.

The largest and finest of residences by Mackintosh is Hill House, near Glasgow, completed in 1903. It is built of local sandstone with a rough finish. Hill House is a large, three-story residence with a rather traditional exterior. It is the interior that is exceptional. Specially designed built-in furniture graces the bedrooms and the entrance hall. Most of the walls are white, some with stencil patterns in pastel colors. Mackintosh designed the furniture, the light fixtures and the fireplace tools. He also landscaped the grounds, and specified that the trees were to be trimmed to match his drawings.

Mackintosh became well known as a designer, and was invited to exhibit in many countries in Europe. He spent the last nine years of his life in the south of France, painting watercolors.

Charles Harrison Townsend 1851–1928

Charles Harrison Townsend's most noteworthy design is the Horniman Museum. Located in South London, the broad, almost windowless facade of the Horniman is joined at the right to a tall clock tower. The tower itself an impressive example of English Art Nouveau. The light stone surface has acquired the usual big-city blight, stained by sixty years of sulfur and carbon, yet the form is still attractive. Inside, the exhibit galleries are well lighted by a large skylight.

Townsend used the Romanesque arch to good advantage in the Whitechapel Art Gallery. The facade is of light stone, mercifully clean, and is distinguished by a large and elaborately detailed Romanesque arch over the entrance doors, an arch half the width of the narrow frontage. A horizontal row of small windows crosses the building's front just above the arch. Originally a large mosaic was planned, to be centered in the upper half of the facade, but it was never begun.

Horniman Museum, South London, 1901. Charles Harrison Townsend. Closest to art nouveau in England were the buildings by Townsend. The clock tower here is four-square and solid, with decoration limited to the stonework at top and bottom. The barrel vault roof of glass and steel brings natural light to the third floor galleries. A mosaic mural by Robert Anning Bell is installed above the street entrance.

Entrance, Whitechapel Art Gallery, London, 1901. Charles Harrison Townsend. The Romanesque arch above the Whitechapel Gallery entrance has almost the same design features as the Horniman Museum entrance arch at the base of the clock tower. Here it is wider and curved inward from the street level to the top. The outer stone edge of the arch ends in small brackets on each side. A multi-paned window lights the lobby.

Antonio Gaudí 1852–1926

Antonio Gaudí was one of the great architects of the twentieth century. His buildings are unusual, flowing, rich designs, with a curving, lively feel. He had a profound understanding and appreciation of engineering. He also had skill amounting to genius as a designer and constructor. His buildings combine innovative structural systems and an imaginative use of materials. Decoration plays a part, but always is subservient to structure. Many architects have some good buildings, one or two great ones and several ordinary ones. This is not so with Gaudí. Almost all of his works are superb, whatever their size.

In 1884 Gaudí was appointed architect in charge of building a large church dedicated to the Holy Family, La Sagrada Familia. This assignment was his principal interest for the rest of his life. By 1893 the walls of the apse were complete, and the first tower was up by 1918. The first spire was not completed until six months after Gaudí's death in 1926. The Nativity portal was finished in 1930, and now, some fifty years later, the portal of the Passion is complete. It may be another hundred years before the church is consecrated, as it is being built stone by stone, and peseta by peseta.

Portal of the Nativity, Church of La Sagrada Familia, Barcelona, Spain, 1884 to present. Antonio Gaudí. *The face shown in this view will be the interior side of the portal when the church is completed. The base is Gothic, below the towers is Spanish art nouveau and the pinnacles are geometric cubism.*

Pinnacle, La Sagrada Familia.

The two portals now complete each have four majestic towers. The upper halves of these contain only a sinuous spiral stairway that is in itself a work of art. Slender and tall, with windows like little eyelids, the towers end in spires that are also works of art. Part painting, part sculpture, ingeniously engineered, they are some of Gaudí's most imaginative creations. Although many of Gaudí's plans were destroyed by Franco's bombers in 1936, enough models were salvaged that the work can go on to completion.

In 1878 Gaudí met Eusebio Güell, a wealthy nobleman who became his friend and patron. Gaudí's first commission was the design of two pavilions for Güell's country estate on the edge of Barcelona, the Finca Güell. These were a gate-keeper's lodge and a stables. The walls of the two buildings combine elaborate brick and tile design with unglazed ceramic castings unique in Gaudí's work. Gaudí used parabolic arches in the exterior windows and for the structural beams supporting the stable roof. The outstanding feature of the Finca Güell pavilions is not the architecture, however, but the wrought iron gate. Gaudí designed this to fit between the two buildings, the so-called "Dragon gate." Gaudí was fond of the dragon as a sculptural motif, and used it many times. The dragon on the gate has an open mouth with protruding tongue, huge talons, spreading wings and a spiral tail. It is one of Gaudí's finest sculptures.

Gaudí had another commission from Eusebio Güell for the organization of a residential park on a hilly site north of Barcelona. This garden suburb was the first of its kind in Spain. Gaudí's solutions were inventive. He constructed covered walkways for pedestrians. The walkway tops were roadways for cars and carriages.

Stairwell, La Sagrada Familia. Each tower of La Sagrada Familia has a spiral staircase of masonry. The carved railings have been nicely polished by thousands of hands over the years.

"Dragon Gate," Finca Güell, Barcelona, 1887. Antonio Gaudí. Gaudí's father was a coppersmith and Gaudí himself enjoyed designing metal gates and railings of singular and fantastic form.

Vaulting, Colonia Güell Chapel Crypt, near Barcelona, 1898-1915. Antonio Gaudí. This unusual vaulting was designed for the crypt of a chapel on the western edge of Barcelona. It forms the ceiling of the crypt and supports the floor above. It was laid up of bricks on edge by skilled Catalan craftsmen. Many vaults in Gaudí's buildings were constructed in the same fashion.

One enters the park through beautiful iron gates placed between two gate houses, one for the porter and the other an office building. These two buildings have the captivating charm of fairy castles; the charm is genuine, not ersatz. Leaving the entrance court, one ascends a double stairway past fantastic dragon and lizard fountains to a covered open space. Its earthen roof is supported by a forest of Doric columns. The top of the roof is a children's playground. Surrounding the playground is an undulating bench faced with the most delightful display of ceramic tile imaginable. Güell Park is unique, a masterpiece comparable to La Sagrada Familia.

Benches, Guell Park. Square Spanish tiles would not fit the irregular surfaces of the Güell Park benches. They are covered instead with a delightful assortment of broken tiles and dishes.

Facade, Casa Battló, Barcelona, 1905-1907. Antonio Gaudí. The facade of the Casa Battló, the "House of Bones" is one of the most sculptural of Gaudí's designs. The sculptural quality continues in the interior, where walls, windows, doors and ceilings are carved or cast in non-conforming shapes.

Facade, Casa Mila, Barcelona, 1905-1910. Antonio Gaudí.

Two very fine late works by Gaudí are the Casa Batlló and the Casa Milá. These are apartment buildings on the Paseo de Gracia, one of Barcelona's most fashionable streets. For these two buildings Gaudí was able to use his own mature solutions to design, ignoring all historical styles.

Street Door, Casa Milá.

Chimneys, Casa Milá. *Gaudí used his sculptural inventiveness in designing Casa Milá's chimneys.*

The owner of the Casa Battló, a textile manufacturer, asked Gaudí to remodel and reface an older building. Gaudí gave the new facade a slightly rippled surface faced in small blue ceramic tiles and dappled with larger round tiles of various colors. Rising from the sidewalk and surrounding the windows on the first floor are curved stone shapes of a most bizarre, bonelike quality. These inspired the local epithet, the "House of Bones." Gaudí added a seventh floor and covered it with a spectacular curving roof-ridge which suggests the backbone of a dragon. The blue-tiled stairwell is striking with its elegantly framed windows and carved mahogany doors.

A few blocks from the Casa Batlló is the Casa Milá, the last of Gaudí's private commissions, completed in 1910. He spent the rest of his life working on La Sagrada Familia. The undulating surface of the Casa Milá is carved in hard stone. It has a wave-like, rock-like appearance that makes it different from any other building in the world. The Barcelonans call it *La Pedrera,* the Stone Quarry. The balconies on the facade have ornamental iron railings of extremely free design. A distinctive feature is the pair of imposing iron-and-glass entrance doors. These are fifteen feet high and equally wide. From inside, the heavy iron framework forms a striking silhouette against the bright sunshine on the Paseo de Gracia. Part of the singular charm of the Casa Milá lies in the undulating surface of the roof and in its exotic chimneys and pinnacles. Atop a short staircase Gaudí designed a little arch to frame a view of La Sagrada Familia in the distance.

Antonio Gaudí lived his whole adult life in Barcelona, working quietly and developing a highly personal style. His work was little known for many decades. It was twenty years after his death before his imaginative use of material and his sculptural inventiveness began to influence modern architecture.

Art Nouveau, as a movement, had a short life. Just as it was itself a reaction against traditional styles, there was, after a few years, a counter-reaction, and even Art Nouveau architects changed their style. For many decades up to the middle of the twentieth century Art Nouveau in general was held in negative judgement by critics and historians. After 1950 a reaction against a rigidly rational architecture emerged. Art Nouveau was re-evaluated and a desire to achieve a more organic harmony with the landscape and the environment became evident.

5

SCHOOLS OF THOUGHT

In the USA and Germany, other movements were establishing themselves at the same time as the iron structures of Gustave Eiffel, the reinforced concrete buildings of Perret and Freyssinet and the Art Nouveau buildings of Horta, Guimard and Wagner were being built.

In Chicago a number of architects specializing in tall commercial buildings became known as the Chicago School. Other architects working in the midwest and in the Chicago suburbs were members of the Prairie School. These were not schools as such, simply architects with similar ideas. In Germany in 1919 the Bauhaus came into being. This was a school in the literal sense, founded by Walter Gropius.

This chapter looks at the architecture of all three groups, whose works helped set the stage for modern architecture.

THE CHICAGO SCHOOL

Chicago began as a cluster of cabins located on a swamp near Lake Michigan. By the end of the Civil War Chicago's population had grown to a quarter of a million.

In forty-eight hours in October of 1871, a devastating fire totally consumed the center third of Chicago. The fire was an enormous disaster, but the reconstruction program gave Chicago's architects a rare opportunity to develop new forms, techniques and styles in building design.

Three important technical advances made it possible to build large, multi-storied, fireproof buildings. **Iron framing** could support tall, light-weight structures. Newly-developed **elevators** made tall buildings practical. **Hollow ceramic tile,** to cover iron supports, made buildings fireproof.

These three innovations presented fresh design challenges. Through U-shaped plans, center courts, and generous windows, Chicago architects brought light into their buildings. Using wide-spanning beams, they made buildings spacious.

William Le Baron Jenney (1832–1907)

The first of the Chicago School architects, and one of the most important, was William Le Baron Jenney. In 1867 he came to Chicago and opened an office, where he employed Louis Sullivan, William Holabird, Martin Roche and Daniel Burnham. All of these men became leading architects of the Chicago School.

Jenney established himself as an architect by designing the first Leiter Building on Monroe Street, completed in 1879. Basically a glass box, the floors and roof loads were carried by joists supported on cast iron columns. Jenney achieved true skeleton construction with the Home Insurance Building of 1885, but the great technical advances of the framing were hidden by an over-decorative facade. In the second Leiter Building, designed with his assistant William Mundie, the facade is restrained and refined. There is a fine interior spaciousness to this building, due to the high ceilings and slender iron columns. The long spandrels and delicate mullions of the exterior proclaim the steel and wrought iron framing.

Taliesin West, Scottsdale, Arizona, 1938. Frank Lloyd Wright. This view of the drafting room shows the redwood beams locked into the rock and concrete walls.

Second Leiter Building, *Chicago, 1891. Jenney and Mundie. The design is simple and direct, with narrow piers indicating the steel construction. Ornament is used sparingly; the building is a good example of Chicago's "commercial style."*

Manhattan Building, *Chicago, 1890. William LeBaron Jenney. This was the first tall office building to use the steel skeleton throughout, an important engineering accomplishment for Jenney. Inventive in structure but not particularly in design, the elements in the facade are too varied for unity.*

Henry Hobson Richardson (1838–1886)

Richardson was not a member of the Chicago School but his warehouse for Marshall Field and his house for John Glessner, both completed in 1887, were of strong influence on other leading architects of Chicago.

Richardson's architectural career began in Boston, where in 1872 he won the competition for the design of Trinity Church. He abandoned the popular Empire and Victorian Gothic styles and began to simplify form, using basic shapes and banded windows. Trinity Church is in the form of a Greek cross, with a tower in the center. Because of the unified pattern of its exterior and the splendid interior space, it is a worthy predecessor of modern architecture. For the next twenty years many American churches were modeled after Trinity Church.

Richardson designed a series of library buildings following his work on Trinity Church. The Thomas Crane Public Library in Quincy, Massachusetts, completed in 1882, is the finest of this group. The building is rectangular, and the reading room, hall and stack space are in line along the main axis. Richardson also designed Harvard University's Sever Hall, using red brick to match the other buildings of Harvard Yard.

Trinity Church, *Boston, 1877. Henry Hobson Richardson. The square tower has corner turrets, a roof of red tiles and is over 200 feet in height. Romanesque arches dominate the door and window openings. Dark and light masonry squares form a pattern above the tall windows.*

Interior, Trinity Church. The ceilings of Trinity are triple barrel vaults. The apse is semi-circular and its floor is several steps higher than the main floor. At each end of the transept is a gallery, with a third gallery at the end of the nave. Between the two towers of the west front is a vestibule.

Thomas Crane Public Library, Quincy, Massachusetts, Henry H. Richardson. Photograph by Tad Goodale. Below the gable is a round entrance arch, and to its left is a circular stair tower. The windows to the left of the entrance are in a horizontal band, and those to the right are in a large two-story-high rectangle. "Eyebrow" windows break up the expanse of the roof.

Sever Hall, Harvard University, 1880. Henry Hobson Richardson. Sever Hall is a large building rectangular in plan. The east and west facades are divided into three sections by semi-cylindrical towers. Foundations and trim are of Longmeadow stone and the roof is covered with red tile. The long dormer lights the attic and adds to the long, low lines of the building.

Marshall Field Wholesale Store, Chicago, 1887. Henry Hobson Richardson. Photograph courtesy the Chicago Historical Society. Exterior walls were of red granite and red sandstone. The almost complete lack of decoration and the simplified rhythm of the window arrangements were an inspiration for architects who followed. Windows for the three floors above the ground floor were in single units with round arches; those for the next floors above were in double units, and the top floor windows were rectangular and in quadruple units. A variation of this window treatment was used a year later by Louis Sullivan in his Auditorium Building.

The Marshall Field Wholesale Store in Chicago was one of Richardson's finest works. The Field building was a solid block of masonry supporting walls seven stories high, with interior piers and floor beams of iron. An interior court brought in needed light. This splendid forerunner of modern architecture was demolished in 1930 to make way for a parking garage.

Glessner House, *Chicago, 1887. Henry Hobson Richardson. The exterior of Glessner House is a simple mass of solid masonry, intended to shut out the city from the open inner court. Carved ornament is used sparingly.*

Courtyard, Glessner House. *The plan of Glessner House is ingeniously arranged in an L around an inner walled courtyard. The high walls of the courtyard shut out the city and give complete privacy. Grime has darkened the bricks but the Joliet limestone lintels remain clean, too white in contrast.*

Side Entrance Door, Glessner House. *This Romanesque entrance arch on Eighteenth Street is a fine example of the simple and effective use of Richardson's favorite form.*

Richardson's second Chicago building, a residence for J.J. Glessner, is still in excellent condition at 18th Street and Prairie Avenue on Chicago's South Side. Mr. Glessner gave Richardson a list of the rooms he wanted and left the design to the architect. Richardson's inventive solution was an L-shaped building arranged around a walled courtyard. The street-side exteriors are plain, with small windows, and the visual effect is one of a massive pile of gray granite.

Two of Richardson's favorite architectural expressions were the Romanesque entrance arch and the semi-cylindrical tower, both of which were used in the Glessner House. Most of the rooms on the first floor face the courtyard, but none of them are very large, due to space priority given the court. After Mr. Glessner's death in 1936 the house passed from one ownership to another and was saved from destruction by the formation of the Chicago Architecture Foundation. This group now owns the building and has restored it and opened it to the public.

Daniel Burnham (1846–1912)/
John Wellborn Root (1850–1891)

In the partnership of Daniel Burnham and John Root, Burnham was the organizer and Root the creative partner. One of their outstanding Chicago buildings still in use is the Rookery, completed in 1886. It is built as a hollow square with an open court in the center giving light to each office. Two charming interior features are the stairways in the light court: on the west side is a suspended stairway and above it a semi-circular one. Above the lobby is a glass and iron dome reminiscent of the glass and iron vaults of European engineers. The windows of the inner walls are in continuous bands, the so-called "ribbon windows" later to be used by Frank Lloyd Wright, Walter Gropius and others.

Burnham and Root also designed the Monadnock Building, completed in 1891. It is totally different from the Rookery. The Monadnock is the tallest building ever constructed with masonry walls. The walls are six feet thick at the base. It is sixteen stories high, very narrow, and from the north, looks like a capital "I." The walls are of smooth stone at the base and of brick above. They slope slightly inward from the top of the first floor.

Monadnock Building, Chicago, 1891. Burnham and Root. The outstanding vertical bays of windows are thirteen stories high, each cantilevered from the base of the third floor.

Rookery Building, Chicago, 1886. Burnham and Root. The facade of the Rookery is distinguished by a strong contrast between its columns and the rugged stonework. Ornament is sparse and carefully placed. The center is emphasized by a gentle bay with attached columns at the upper stories.

Rookery Building Stairwell. The white marble steps of the graceful Rookery stairwell contrast elegantly with the dark metal railings. A simple flower-like ornament decorates the railings.

Reliance Building, *Chicago, 1895. D.H. Burnham and Company. The Reliance in its day came close to Mies van der Rohe's later dreams of an all-glass skyscraper (see p. 78), although Mies was only nine when the Reliance was completed.*

Railway Exchange Building, *Chicago, 1904. D.H. Burnham and Company. One of many Chicago buildings completed by Burnham and Company, the Railway Exchange has a facade of gleaming white terra cotta tiles lightly ornamented. Projecting bays create a restful rhythm along the street sides.*

When John Root died in 1891, Daniel Burnham carried on as D.H. Burnham and Company. One of the finest of this firm's buildings is the Reliance Building on State Street. The Reliance Building was designed by Charles Atwood and engineered by Edward Shankland. Today it appears to be merely an office building jammed in among others, disfigured by tasteless signs and badly in need of cleaning. Yet when it was built it was a light, airy, nearly all-glass building, its slender spandrels and delicate piers clad in gleaming light ceramic tiles.

William Holabird (1854–1923)/
Martin Roche (1853–1927)
William Holabird and Martin Roche became partners in 1883. Together they built some of the outstanding office buildings of dowtown Chicago. The Marquette Building is one of their finest structures. It incorporates a masterly use of steel framing with a finely proportioned exterior. The facade is simple and harmonious, with large rectangular windows giving a maximum amount of light to each office. The plan is E-shaped, with the center bar of the "E" serving as a generous elevator lobby for each floor.

Marquette Building, Chicago, 1894. Holabird and Roche.

Lobby, Marquette Building. Colorful mosaics in the ground floor lobby are by Tiffany Studios.

Montgomery Ward and
Company Warehouse,
*Chicago, 1907.
Schmidt, Garden and
Martin.*

Richard Schmidt (1865–1958)/
Hugh Garden (1873–1961)/
Edgar Martin (1871–1951)

Richard Schmidt, Hugh Garden and Edgar Martin formed a partnership in 1906. Their first commission was the largest in their twenty-year partnership, a warehouse for mail order tycoon A. Montgomery Ward. Located on the north branch of the Chicago River, it is the largest building of the Chicago School built on a reinforced concrete frame. The floor space alone is almost 160,000 square feet. The facade reveals the structure, and projecting bands at top and bottom of each spandrel emphasize the horizontal. The Wards' Warehouse is a distinguished example of utilitarian architecture.

THE PRAIRIE SCHOOL

A second group of architects, many of whom worked in Chicago or its suburbs, became known as the Prairie School. Various names have been given this group— the Second Chicago School, the Suburban Chicago School, the School of the Middle West. Thanks to writers H. Allen Brooks, William Hasbrouck and others, the name "Prairie School" is now the accepted one. The emphasis in this school was not on tall office buildings but primarily on residences and banks on the prairies of the midwest.

Membership in "schools" tends to be nebulous; the "member" is not always aware that he is indeed a member. Louis Sullivan is seen by many historians as having been a member of both the Chicago School in his early skyscraper buildings and the Prairie School in his buildings in the Midwest after 1900.

Louis Henry Sullivan (1856–1924)

Louis Henry Sullivan was born in Boston and came to Chicago in 1873. The city still lay largely in ruins, but building activity was brisk. Sullivan went to work for William Le Baron Jenney. In 1879 he was hired by Dankmar Adler, and was made partner in 1881. Sullivan soon became the leading architect in Chicago. He became known and admired for his writings, his theories and his humanist approach to his profession.

Sullivan's insistence that "form follows function" explained his belief that a forthright expression of use and structure was a necessary precondition for a beautiful building. He influenced modern architecture with the simplicity of his facades and the striking forms he found for tall office buildings, based on steel cages.

The most notable commission for Adler and Sullivan was the Auditorium Building on Michigan Avenue. In the very simplicity of its Michigan Avenue facade, in its absence of ornament, with its heavy columns and huge granite blocks, the Auditorium is a truly monumental building. Three large round arches form the entrance doorways on Michigan Avenue, and three smaller but higher arches offer entrance to the theater on Congress Parkway. Above the entrances on Michigan is a cantilevered balcony with six immense plate glass windows.

The exterior of the Auditorium is impressive, but the really striking part of the building is the theater. Sullivan was responsible for the spectacular architectural effect, and Adler for the acoustical perfection and the faultless seating arrangement. The proscenium arch is an elegant curve. Above it is a large mural. On the ceiling is a series of four elliptical arches, which were scientifically designed to improve the acoustics.

Interior, Auditorium Theater, Grand Reopening Night, 1967. The arches are covered with gold leaf and studded with small, carbon-filament electric lights. The whole effect is of a shimmering golden glow.

Auditorium Building, *Chicago, 1889. Adler and Sullivan. The exterior design of the Auditorium, with its vertical rows of recessed windows topped by Romanesque arches, clearly shows the influence of H.H. Richardson's Marshall Field Wholesale Store.*

Wainwright Building, *St. Louis, 1891. Adler and Sullivan.*

James Charnley Residence, *Chicago, 1892. Adler and Sullivan.*

In the six years following the Auditorium Adler and Sullivan designed nearly forty buildings. The Wainwright Building in St. Louis was Adler and Sullivan's first skyscraper, completed in 1892, with a height of 135 feet. The building is U-shaped and framed entirely in steel. This provides outside light for every office. The piers between the windows are boldly vertical and the exterior is lavishly ornamental. The full twelve-foot exterior of the top floor is covered with a rich pattern of carved foliage.

The Charnley House in Chicago followed the Wainwright Building. Credit for the design usually is divided between Louis Sullivan and Frank Lloyd Wright whose work is discussed next. He was working for Sullivan when the Charnley House was built. It is a blocky, monumental building clad in yellow Roman brick. The cantilevered balcony with its ornamental railing probably is Sullivan's, but the entrance bay arrangement apparently is Wright's, as he repeated it a year later in his Winslow House in River Forest.

One of Sullivan's notable building designs was for the Transportation Building, a temporary structure for the World's Columbian Exposition of 1893. One of the largest buildings of the Fair, it covered five and one-half acres. The long walls were flat, and painted in brilliant colors. The most noteworthy feature was the massive "Golden Door," an enormous Romanesque gateway of five concentric arches, each covered partly with gold leaf. A wide ornamented border framed the arches. A bold cornice topped the whole.

The depression of 1893 was hard on architects especially, and led to the dissolution of the Adler-Sullivan partnership. Sullivan's most important and most distinctive building was begun in 1899, in Chicago. It was commissioned by Schlesinger and Mayer for a department store, but was sold to Carson, Pirie Scott and Company before it was completed in 1904. This building represents the first truly mature form of the steel framed skyscraper. The interior is an unbroken floor space for display of merchandise, and the floor-to-ceiling windows are the most refined of the "Chicago" windows, each with a large fixed center pane and tall, narrow, hinged windows on each side.

"Golden Door," entrance to Transportation Building, *World's Columbian Exposition, 1893. Adler and Sullivan. Photograph by C.D. Arnold, courtesy Chicago Historical Society.*

Carson Pirie Scott Store, *formerly Schlesinger and Mayer Store, Chicago, 1904. Louis Sullivan. The exterior of Carson's is plain, except the first two floors. These are exceptionally rich in cast iron ornament detailed by George Elmslie and modeled by Kristian Schneider, both of whom had worked for Sullivan for a long time.*

Detail over Main Entrance, Carson Pirie Scott Store.

Interior, National Farmers' Bank, Owatonna, Minnesota, *1908. Louis Sullivan. Photograph courtesy Northwestern Bank, Owatonna, Minnesota. The two great half-round windows on the street side are thirty-six feet in diameter, of opalescent leaded glass.*

The last and most interesting of Sullivan's designs in his later years were a series of small-town banks in the midwest. The first and most impressive of these banks is the National Farmers' Bank in Owatonna, Minnesota, completed in 1908. It has a simple cube shape with handsome decoration, much of it by George Elmslie. Other bank commissions followed—the People's Savings Bank in Cedar Rapids, and banks in Wisconsin, Ohio and Iowa. But Sullivan's commissions were not enough to pay his bills, and he died literally penniless in Chicago in April of 1924. He is buried in Graceland Cemetery; his modest gravestone was provided by his friends.

Frank Lloyd Wright (1867–1959)

As a young man Frank Lloyd Wright worked for a contractor and studied civil engineering at the University of Wisconsin. Before graduating, he left to go to work in Chicago, where he worked first for J.L. Silsbee, then for Adler and Sullivan. In 1893 he left Adler and Sullivan to begin his own practice in Oak Park, Illinois.

Wright's first outstanding house was the Winslow House in River Forest, Illinois. His preference for the horizontal was first stated here. The first floor is a long, low band of warm-toned Roman brick and carved limestone. Above it, the second story is a long band of brown ornamental tiles. The Winslow House is a masterpiece, yet Wright was only twenty-five when he designed it.

With the turn of the century Wright embarked on a series of extraordinary houses which came to be known as the Prairie Houses. One of the finest of these is the Ward Willits House in Highland Park, Illinois, completed in 1902. The Willits House is shaped like a cross, with three fireplaces at the center, for kitchen, dining room and living room.

A second handsome house of 1902 is the Huertley House in Oak Park, Illinois. It has a long, low profile. The red-brown Roman brick is unusually fine, laid in alternating rows of varying depth. The entrance doorway is a Roman arch of carefully tapered brick. Patterned-glass windows are set in a band directly under the roof overhang to keep the long, low look.

A complex and exceptionally well-designed house was built for the Avery Coonleys in Riverside, Illinois in 1908. The Coonley House has many of the qualities of a small palace, including sumptuous living quarters, an elegant terrace, and a large swimming pool. The walls are stucco with orange and brown ceramic tiles.

The best of Wright's Prairie Houses is the Robie House, completed in 1909 on Chicago's south side. It is built on a narrow lot, with two long overlapping rectangles. Once destined for demolition, the Robie House has been carefully restored and is now part of the University of Chicago.

Winslow House, *River Forest, Illinois, 1893.*
Frank Lloyd Wright.

Ward Willits House, *Highland Park, Illinois,*
1902. Frank Lloyd Wright.

Arthur Heurtley House, *Oak Park, Illinois,*
1902. Frank Lloyd Wright.

Robie House, *Chicago, Illinois, 1909. Frank*
Lloyd Wright. Everything in Wright's design
contributes to the feeling of stretched-out
horizontality: the sweeping cantilevers of the
roof at each end, the unbroken roof line and
balcony rails, even the long, narrow Roman
bricks.

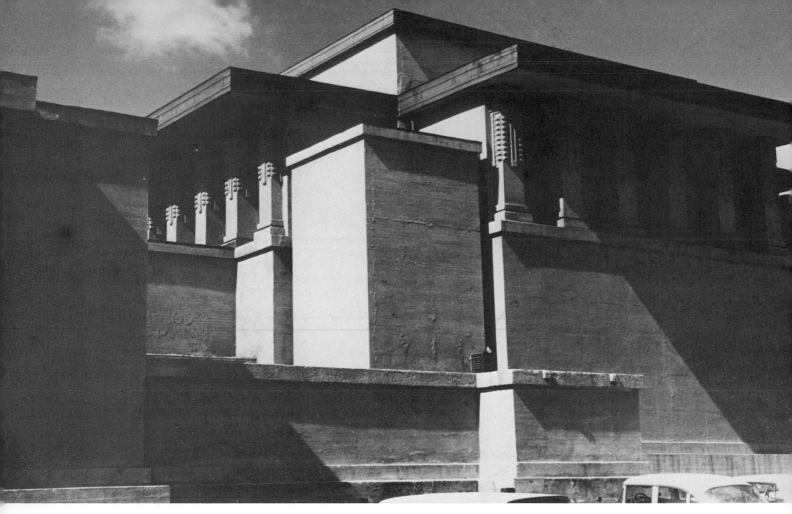

Unity Church, Oak Park, Illinois, 1906. Frank Lloyd Wright. Blocky and stocky, Unity Church has influenced many later buildings in America and Europe.

While working on the Prairie Houses, Wright also designed a new church for his Unitarian congregation in Oak Park. Unity Church, completed in 1906, was one of the first poured-concrete buildings in the United States. The building is H-shaped, with the church area on one side and the parish house on the other. An entrance lobby and reception area connect the two. The auditorium is small, with a feeling of intimacy. The roofs are concrete slabs, and stained glass skylights illuminate the church and the entrance area.

In 1911, Wright built a home on family-owned land near Spring Green, Wisconsin. He named it Taliesin, or "Shining Brow" in the Welsh of his ancestors. A few years later, a berserk servant at Taliesin killed Wright's companion, Mrs. Cheney, her two children and four workmen, and set fire to the building. After this disaster, Wright struggled to survive and was helped by receiving a commission to go to Tokyo and design and build the Imperial Hotel. The Imperial Hotel was carefully engineered, with specially designed "floating" foundations to resist earthquake damage. Some parts of the building were designed to a small scale—some doors, for instance, were only five feet high—yet the Imperial Hotel was one of the grandest, most impressive buildings in Tokyo. In the mid-seventies the Imperial Hotel was demolished to make way for a new high-rise hotel.

Imperial Hotel, *Tokyo, 1922. Frank Lloyd Wright. Photograph by Elizabeth Stein. The ornament was often reminiscent of Mayan or American Indian themes, yet the engineering so superb that the hotel was one of the very few Tokyo buildings to survive the terrible earthquake of 1923.*

Taliesin III, *near Spring Green, Wisconsin, 1925. Frank Lloyd Wright.*

Wright returned to Wisconsin, only to have his second home, Taliesin II, burn to the ground. In 1925, he began Taliesin III, which still stands amid the rolling hills of southern Wisconsin. Taliesin III is built of native limestone, with low hipped roofs of cedar shingles and with overhanging eaves. It was Wright's refuge for many years.

When Wright was in his late sixties, at the age when most men retire, he began the second half of his architectural career. Within a few short years he designed the Kaufmann House, "Falling Water," at Bear Run, Pennsylvania, the Johnson Wax Administration Building in Racine, Wisconsin and his winter home, Taliesin West, near Scottsdale, Arizona.

Kaufmann House, Falling Water, *Connellsville, Pennsylvania. Frank Lloyd Wright. Falling Water at Bear Run is pure poetry—the daring cantilevered balconies are anchored into a rocky ledge, and balanced by vertical piers of local stone, quarried almost at the site.*

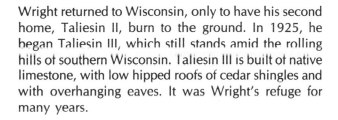

Interior, Johnson Wax Administration Building.

The Johnson Wax Building is Wright's outstanding major building, the culmination of his creative powers, begun the same year as the Kaufmann House. It is warm and handsome on the exterior, but it is the great work room inside which gives it its grandeur. Vincent Scully Jr., in his book, *Frank Lloyd Wright*, describes the tulip columns: ''They stand as if growing and floating in the quietest space of all, a deep and limpid pool.''

Johnson Wax Administration Building, *Racine, Wisconsin, 1939. Frank Lloyd Wright. Photograph courtesy S.E. Johnson and Son.*

Goetsch-Winkler House, *Okemos, Michigan, 1939. Frank Lloyd Wright. In the late 1930's Wright designed several inexpensive wood-framed residences he called his "Usonian" houses. The Goetsch-Winkler House is one of the finest. In its low profile, broadly cantilevered carport roof and simple, unornamented lines, it is the true progenitor of the ranch house.*

Solomon R. Guggenheim Museum, *New York, 1959. Frank Lloyd Wright.*

Wright's third great achievement of his later years was his home in the desert—Taliesin West (see p. 52). For this extraordinary complex of buildings he invented a new material: "desert rock." To form the walls, plywood forms were erected, filled with rocks of different colors, and concrete poured in to hold the rocks in place.

Wright's last major building was the Guggenheim Museum in New York City, completed the year of his death in 1959. This is an interesting, exciting, and controversial building, praised by some and condemned by others. The Guggenheim Museum is in the form of a giant concrete spiral ramp which makes five complete turns as it rises upward and slightly outward around a central open area. A large glass dome brings light to the interior, where visitors can, as one of my students wrote, "look at the paintings as they walk down the ramp."

During seventy years of work, Frank Lloyd Wright completed hundreds of buildings. Some of his outstanding architectural innovations were deeply cantilevered, long low roofs, patterned glass windows (each now a museum piece) and the open plan ("breaking up the box" as he put it). His work also included a search for new materials as in the Guggenheim and the Johnson's Wax Building, imaginative floor plans and superb siting of his residences as in the Taliesins and Falling Water. In the quarter-century since his death, Wright's reputation as an architect has gone steadily upward. It is not likely we shall see another architect of his ability again in this century.

George W. Maher (1864–1926)

Much of Mahers' work showed a preference for blocky, symmetrical design, as in the John Farson House in Oak Park, Illinois. The Farson House is almost exactly bisymmetrical, with the facade divided into thirds. In this respect it is reminiscent of Frank Lloyd Wright's Winslow House of four years earlier, even to the tiled hip roof and the bowl-shaped planters on each side of the entrance.

The Taylor House is the last of Maher's Oak Park houses, and like the Farson House it is evenly symmetrical. It is of yellow brick, with a stone entranceway, and has a flat facade with large windows on each side and six narrow casement windows in a band over the entrance. Above the doorway is a flattened arch.

F.N. Corbin House, *Kenilworth, Illinois, 1904. George W. Maher.*

John Farson House, *Oak Park, Illinois, 1897. George W. Maher.*

James Taylor House, *Oak Park, Illinois, 1906. George W. Maher. Maher's avowed aim in creating residential architecture was "massiveness and substantiality," and he often succeeded in reaching it.*

William Drummond (1876–1948)

William Drummond moved to Chicago from New Jersey in 1884, and as a young man worked for both Louis Sullivan in Chicago and Frank Lloyd Wright in Oak Park. An early Drummond building was the First Congregational Church in Austin on Chicago's west side. The facade is bold and vigorous, with three tall stained glass windows set deeply between wide brick piers. A low, dark entrance leads one into a high nave, brightly skylighted in stained glass.

Following the Austin church Drummond designed his own home in River Forest, located next to Wright's Isabelle Roberts House. The exterior of the Drummond House is of wood and stucco, with trim. The upper floor is cantilevered several feet on each side. A huge brick fireplace is the central feature of the living room.

William E. Drummond House, *River Forest, Illinois, 1910. William E. Drummond.*

Thorncroft, *House for Mrs. Avery Coonley, Riverside, Illinois, 1910. William E. Drummond.*

In 1912 Drummond formed a partnership with Louis Guenzel. One of their first commissions was the River Forest Women's Club, designed by Drummond. This is a well-planned building sheathed in horizontal boards and battens. Also designed by Drummond was the Ralph S. Baker House in Wilmette. This is a sharply angular building typical of Drummond's residential designs.

River Forest Women's Club, *River Forest, Illinois, 1913. Louis Guenzel and William Drummond. Cantilevered roof slabs project over the entrance and the front of the building. Clerestory windows light the auditorium.*

Ralph Baker House, *Wilmette, Illinois, 1914. Louis Guenzel and William Drummond. The slab roofs are of varying heights and the windows are set in bands. The two-story living room has balconies on three sides. It is illuminated by large clerestory windows on the street side.*

Walter Burley Griffin (1876–1937)/
Marion Mahony Griffin (1871–1962)

One of the leading members of the Prairie School was Walter Burley Griffin, who went to work for Frank Lloyd Wright in 1901. One of Griffin's notable early buildings was a home for William Emery in Elmhurst, Illinois, completed in 1902 while he was working for Wright. Spaces flow logically, and rooms are provided for all the niceties of suburban living. The interior is a series of split levels, and the exterior is white stucco with the windows in broad bands framed in dark wood. Bold brick piers stand at each corner.

Griffin married architect Marion Mahony in 1911. Mahony had worked for Wright in Oak Park and was one of the world's masters of architectural drawing.

In 1912, with the help of Mrs. Griffin's splendid renderings, Griffin won a world-wide competition for the design and layout of Canberra, the capital city of Australia. On the main boulevard of Canberra, the Capitol and Parliament buildings face a broad landscape pool, a lawn, a lake renamed Lake Burley Griffin, and, at the end of the axis, Mount Ainslie. Two primary roads radiate from the capitol. One leads due north between two mountains and the other leads toward Pleasant Hill. When the heavy task of designing Canberra was complete, the Griffins made their home in Australia, where Walter designed many residences and commercial and public buildings.

William Emery House, *Elmhurst, Illinois, 1902. Walter Burley Griffin.*

William Sloan House, *Elmhurst, Illinois, 1909. Walter Burley Griffin. Not far from the Emery House on Arlington Avenue is Griffin's house for William B. Sloan, completed in 1909. Here the central cubic mass is flanked by low wings, with one unbroken horizontal lower roof line uniting the three. The windows are in groups and ornamented with dark wood trim.*

Rendering of Griffin's two houses in Evanston for Hurd Comstock. Marion Mahony Griffin. Photograph courtesy Northwestern University.

The architects of the Chicago School and the Prairie School were some of the twentieth century pioneers of American architecture. Inspired by the genius of Wright and Sullivan, their influence spread far beyond Chicago and the midwest. There were remarkably gifted architects on the West Coast as well, but nowhere else in America was there such a concentration of architectural talent as in the Chicago area.

Walter Burley Griffin's design for the house "Solid Rock," Kenilworth, Illinois, 1911. Rendering by Marion Mahony Griffin. Photograph courtesy Northwestern University.

Aerial view of Canberra, Australia. City plan by Walter Burley Griffin. Photograph courtesy Australian Information Service.

THE BAUHAUS

The Bauhaus, in Germany, was originally an arts and crafts school. Under the leadership of Walter Gropius, it became a center for creative thought in fine art, architecture, furniture and industrial design. From 1919 until it was disbanded in 1933, the Bauhaus brought together many talented and eloquent artists. This heady atmosphere produced a wealth of designs, many of which are now considered classics. This section looks at the Bauhaus influence on architectural design.

Bauhaus Building, *Dessau, Germany, 1926. Walter Gropius. Photograph courtesy Bauhaus-Archiv, Berlin.*

Walter Gropius (1883–1969)

Walter Gropius was the son of an architect. In 1911, with architect Adolf Meyer, he built his first and one of his finest buildings, the Fagus Shoe-Last Factory in Alfeld, Germany. The Fagus Factory is in mint condition today, and with its steel skeleton, cantilevered floors, all-glass facade, and glass-butted corner windows it is so modern-looking it is hard to believe it was built more than seventy years ago.

During the next few years Gropius designed a variety of products, ranging from sleeping-car interiors and a diesel locomotive to a deluxe automobile body for the Adler Company. In 1914, again with Adolf Meyer, he completed the office building for the Werkbund Exhibition in Cologne. This glass-walled building was an astounding success. At each end of the facade circular staircases with cantilevered stairs led to a covered roof terrace and restaurant.

In 1919 Gropius was asked to assume the directorship of the Grand Ducal School of Arts and Crafts of Saxe-Weimar. Wisely, he changed the name to the "Bauhaus" (House of Building). The curriculum and principles of the Bauhaus, as developed under Gropius, have influenced art and design education throughout the world. The Bauhaus curriculum involved instruction in working stone, wood, metal, clay, glass, pigments and textile looms. These were combined with the study of nature, materials, geometry, construction, drawing, color and composition.

In 1925 the mayor of Dessau, Germany, offered Gropius and the Bauhaus a new home and money for new buildings. The move was made, and Gropius designed the new buildings, which were some of his most distinctive and functional structures. The three buildings are a modified pin wheel in plan, with a bridge containing administrative offices connecting the workshop wing and the student dormitory to the classroom building. The buildings are starkly white and rectangular, with no roof cornices or overhangs, and the windows are in dark bands. The Dessau Bauhaus buildings are almost perfect examples of what Alfred Barr of the Museum of Modern Art in New York called the "International Style."

Bauhaus Building, *Workshop Wing, 1926. Walter Gropius. Photograph courtesy Bauhaus-Archiv, Berlin.*

Fagus Factory, *Alfeld a.d. Leine, Germany, 1911. Walter Gropius (with Adolf Meyer).*

Gropius House, *Bauhaus Faculty Housing, 1925. Walter Gropius. Photograph courtesy Bauhaus-Archiv, Berlin.*

Walter Gropius House, *Lincoln, Massachusetts, 1937. Walter Gropius and Marcel Breuer. Photograph by Robert Damora. Interior and exterior spaces are interpenetrating. Projecting roofs shelter the balcony. Narrow wood sheathing reflects local tradition, as does the screened-in porch. This first American house by Gropius reflects his houses for the Bauhaus faculty, but is more open and inviting.*

Tired of attacks from right-wing elements, Gropius resigned as director of the Bauhaus in 1928, and returned to private practice. His first commission was for a large apartment block at Siemenstadt, Germany, and in 1930 he designed the German Exhibition at the Grand Palais in Paris. In 1934, Gropius and his wife Ise were able to leave Germany on the pretext of his lecturing in Rome, but it was really a means of escaping Nazi Germany. They went into exile in England, where Gropius became a partner to architect Maxwell Fry.

In 1937 Gropius was invited to come to America and teach at Harvard. He accepted, and as Chairman of the School of Architecture he had a considerable influence on many young students who later became leading architects, including Paul Rudolph, Philip Johnson and I.M. Pei. Gropius invited Marcel Breuer to come to Harvard as his assistant, and they formed an architectural partnership. Their first building was a house for Gropius at Lincoln, near Boston. It is a relatively simple frame building with a screened-in porch and vertical siding painted white—modern but very New England.

Gropius chaired Harvard's Architecture School for fifteen years. In 1945 he and several of his former students formed the Architects Collaborative, or TAC, which has become an important American architectural firm. Their first large commission was for the Harvard Graduate Center. These buildings are eminently practical spaces built on a tight budget, but comfortable and well-designed.

Harvard Graduate Center, *Cambridge, Massachusetts, 1949. Walter Gropius, with The Architects Collaborative.*

U.S. Embassy, *Athens, Greece, 1961. Walter Gropius and H.*
Morse Payne, The Architects Collaborative. Photograph
courtesy U.S. State Department, Washington, D.C.

Entrance, U.S. Embassy, Athens. Photograph courtesy
U.S. State Department, Washington, D.C.

With Gropius in charge, TAC built the U.S. Embassy
Building in Athens, Greece. This is a serene, stately,
three-story building of reinforced concrete covered with
white Pentellic marble.

Walter Gropius lived a long and fruitful life. He was
given honorary degrees by Harvard, Columbia and
other American universities, as well as universities in
Brazil, Germany and Australia. During his life he
received the gold medals of the Royal Institute of British
Architects and the American Institute of Architects. Fine
architect that he was, his fame will ever rest on his founding and directing of the Bauhaus.

Glass skyscraper, model, 1922. Mies van der Rohe. Photograph courtesy Akademie der Kunste, Berlin.

Ludwig Mies van der Rohe (1886–1969)

Born Ludwig Mies, he later added his mother's surname and became Ludwig Mies van der Rohe. In 1913 he opened his own architecture office in Berlin. Mies van der Rohe had his own design approach. It resembled in three dimensions the paintings of his friend Piet Mondrian: lines vertical and horizontal, all angles at ninety degrees.

During the First World War, jobs were scarce, so Mies developed a series of projects, some of which later brought him fame. One of the most impressive is a project for a thirty-story glass skyscraper. We are used to such buildings today. Almost every large city has one. But Mies' proposal was made in 1920, when Renaissance and Neo-Classical were the popular architectural styles.

In 1929 Mies designed one of his most famous buildings, the German Pavilion for an exposition in Barcelona, Spain. This was a small, one-story building. It had walls of travertine marble, green Tinian marble, and one whole wall of onyx. Other walls were of gray glass, etched glass, and bottle-green glass. The pool was lined with black glass. This elegant building had no doors or windows, just a flat roof slab which rested on the walls, allowing free passage in and out.

German Pavilion, *International Exposition. Barcelona, Spain, 1929. Mies van der Rohe. Photograph courtesy Mies van der Rohe Archive, Museum of Modern Art, New York. This building was taken down in sections, put away, and is now being rebuilt.*

Lake Point Tower, *Chicago, 1968. Schipporeit-Heinrich Associates.*

In 1930 Mies built the Tugendhat house in Brno, Czechoslovakia. Damaged during World War II, the Tugendhat was a brilliant solution to residential design. It had private areas, such as bedrooms, dressing rooms and kitchen. In other ways it resembled the Barcelona Pavilion. Its free-standing walls provided free-flowing space within the large living area. Straight walls were of tawny gold and white onyx. The curved dining room wall was of Macassar ebony. The curtains were raw silk and the drapes were white velvet.

At the suggestion of Walter Gropius, Mies was appointed director of the Bauhaus School at Dessau, Germany in 1930. Mies moved the school to Berlin, but he closed it in 1933 due to pressure from the Nazis. A few years later he left for America.

In 1938, he was appointed Director of Architecture at Armour Institute, which became the Illinois Institute of Technology in 1940. Mies designed nearly all of the new buildings on the I.I.T. campus. The most striking one is Crown Hall, which houses architecture and design.

Crown Hall, above grade, is a large glass box. The roof is supported by lofty I-beams which carry the whole weight. This makes interior walls or columns unnecessary. On the exterior, a broad flight of steps leads to a wide "floating" terrace. From there a second wide stairway leads to the entrance doors. The walls are entirely of glass, set between narrow steel piers.

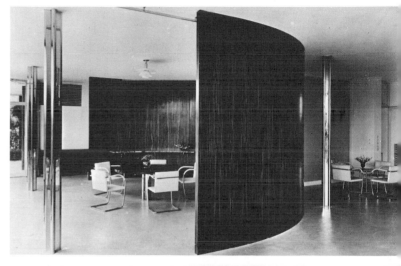

Tugendhat House, Brno, Czechoslovakia, 1930. Dining room. Mies van der Rohe. Photograph courtesy Mies van der Rohe Archive, Museum of Modern Art, New York.

Crown Hall, Illinois Institute of Technology, Chicago. Mies van der Rohe. Photograph courtesy Bill Engdahl, Hedrich-Blessing. With its high ceiling and unbroken space, Crown Hall is a beautiful building which is perhaps more appropriate for a museum or gallery than for classroom use.

Mies was busy at I.I.T. for twenty years, teaching and designing campus buildings. He was also able to accept many other commissions. One of his most graceful buildings is the home he completed for Dr. Edith Farnsworth in Plano, Illinois in 1950. Built near the Fox River, the house is a glass-walled box resting on slim white-painted steel columns. Broad stairs lead to a sizable terrace, which also seems to float, half-way from porch to ground.

Two of the finest and most distinctive of Mies' Chicago apartment buildings are those completed in 1951 at 860 and 880 Lake Shore Drive. They are twin towers of twenty-six stories each, set at an angle to Lake Shore Drive and at a right angle to each other. The entrance lobbies are quietly distinctive, floored with travertine marble and furnished with Mies-designed Barcelona chairs and matching tables. The location is superb, right on the shore of Lake Michigan.

In 1958 Mies completed his best known large building, the Seagram Building on Park Avenue in New York. This is an impressive thirty-nine-story building set well back from a large plaza. Its gray glass and dark bronze mullions lend it a stark but attractive simplicity. Mies' partner in the Seagram planning was Philip Johnson, who went on to become a leading American architect.

Farnsworth House, *Plano, Illinois, 1950. Mies van der Rohe. Mies' Farnsworth House is the outstanding example of his American residential designs. A glass-enclosed volume floats between roof and floor slabs raised five feet above the ground. Eight steel columns spaced twenty-two feet apart support the structure. The entry platform, the steps, the terrace and the interior floor are all faced in white marble. Photograph courtesy Hedrich Blessing, Chicago.*

860-880 Lake Shore Drive Apartments, *Chicago, 1951. Mies van der Rohe. Photograph courtesy Hedrich-Blessing, Chicago.*

Seagram Building, *New York, 1958. Mies van der Rohe.*

The Miesian design influence has been prevalent for three reasons: Post-and-beam constructions can be put together by any good contractor. Glass curtain-walls are easily combined with other surface materials. And glass curtain-walls have been cheaper than masonry or just about any other walls.

Mies was not a writer, yet his aphorisms have entered our language. The most famous of these, given as advice, is, "Less is more." Anyone sitting in a full Victorian parlor understands that. Another phrase used to describe the intentional simplicity and modesty of his I.I.T. buildings is *beinahe nichts*, "almost nothing."

In an early magazine article, he wrote, "Reinforced concrete structures are skeletons by nature . . . columns and girders eliminate bearing walls. This is skin and bone construction." "Skin and bones" has become part of our architectural language, used with affection to describe the great contributions of Ludwig Mies van der Rohe.

New National Gallery, *Berlin, Germany, 1968. Mies van der Rohe. Photograph courtesy Inter Nationes, Bonn, Germany.*

United States Post Office, *part of the Federal Center, Chicago, 1964-1975. Mies van der Rohe; Schmidt, Garden and Erikson; C.F. Murphy Associates; A. Epstein and Sons.*

IBM Building, *Chicago, 1971. Office of Mies van der Rohe and C.F. Murphy Associates. Photograph courtesy Scribner and Co., Chicago. This was the last office building designed by Mies van der Rohe. It is on a K-shaped riverfront site. Just to the west are the cylindrical towers of Marina City, designed by Bertrand Goldberg Associates.*

Marcel Breuer (1902–1981)

Marcel Breuer was born in southern Hungary and studied at the Bauhaus. He became involved with furniture design, and in 1924 Gropius appointed him director of that department. While at the Bauhaus, Breuer invented tubular steel furniture. Fascinated by the chrome plated handle bars of his new bicycle, he decided tubular metal would be ideal for furniture. He proceeded to make the first chrome-plated steel chair. In 1928 he produced a cantilevered steel chair with caned seat and back that is now a classic.

Breuer left Germany in 1935 to become a partner of English architect F.R.S. Yorke. While in England he developed a fine bent-plywood chair, the ''Isokon'' chair.

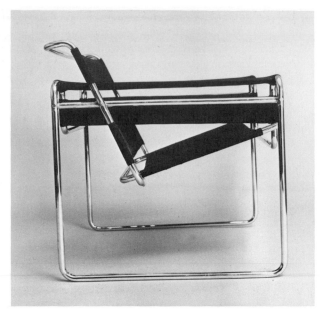

First Tubular Steel Chair *(Club Armchair), late 1927. Marcel Breuer. Chrome-plated tubular steel with canvas slings. Photograph Museum of Modern Art, New York.*

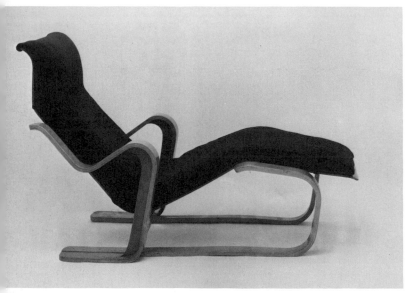

Isokon Reclining Chair, *London, 1935. Marcel Breuer. Laminated bent birch plywood; upholstered pad. 31 1/2" × 53". Photograph Museum of Modern Art, New York.*

When Gropius went to Harvard in 1937 he invited Breuer to join him. They taught together and became architectural partners as well. Breuer's home in Lincoln, Massachusetts was one of the finest of his series of residences designed with Gropius. This house features a two-story living room with the entire fireplace wall made of fieldstone. On the exterior, fieldstone is also used in the chimney and the porch parapet.

Breuer House I, *Lincoln, Massachusetts, 1939. Walter Gropius and Marcel Breuer. Photograph by Ezra Stoller © ESTO.*

Breuer House II, *New Canaan, Connecticut, 1947. Marcel Breuer. Photograph by Robert Damora.*

Breuer later built two more houses for himself, both in New Canaan, Connecticut. The first was completed in 1947 and the second four years later. Breuer House I in New Canaan is cantilevered in all directions from a white-painted concrete base. The cantilevers are achieved without steel beams. The house is wood frame construction throughout. The walls are largely of glass, with some of vertical or diagonal wood siding. The longest cantilevered unit is the balcony. This is supported by standard marine tension cables. Fieldstone walls add diversity to the textures.

Breuer won an important commission in 1953, to design the UNESCO (United Nations Educational, Scientific and Cultural Organization) Headquarters in Paris, in collaboration with famous Italian engineer Pier Luigi Nervi (see Part III) and French architect Bernard Zehrfuss. This large complex has since become famous as the introduction of Breuer to the world. The two buildings of UNESCO are the Y-shaped Secretariat, eight stories tall, and the wedge-shaped Conference Building. Breuer and Nervi were able to work together in harmony and produced a pair of buildings notable for their beauty and usefulness. The end walls as well as the butterfly roof of the Conference Building are folded slabs of reinforced concrete. Half of each side wall is smooth concrete. The other halves are glass.

UNESCO Headquarters, *Paris, 1958. Marcel Breuer, Pier Luigi Nervi, Bernard Zehrfuss. Photograph courtesy UNESCO, D. Berretty. The Secretariat rests on seventy-two Nervi-designed columns and has a Nervi hyperbolic concrete canopy protecting the main entrance.*

Breuer also designed a large church for the Benedictine monks of St. John's Abbey and University in Collegeville, Minnesota. Standing in front of the church is a ten-story bell-banner. This is a huge vertical sheet of concrete supported on parabolic concrete arches. It is pierced to hold the bells of the old monastery. This vertical slab reflects sunlight into the stained glass windows of the church.

St. John's Abbey, Collegeville, Minnesota, 1953-1970. Marcel Breuer with Hamilton Smith. Photograph by Stanley Wold. The church structure is virtually a reprise of the UNESCO Conference Building, with its folded slab concrete walls and roof.

IBM Complex, Boca Raton, Florida, 1977. Marcel Breuer with R.F. Gatje. Photograph by Joseph Molitor, courtesy Marcel Breuer and Associates.

A third Breuer building was De Bijenkorf, the "Beehive" Department Store in Rotterdam. It was completed in 1957 as part of a new postwar city center. Built in the form of a large block, its facade is travertine marble in a honeycomb pattern. Next to the store is an eighty-foot abstract sculpture by Naum Gabo.

Breuer designed two large building complexes for the IBM company, one in the south of France, near Nice, and the other in Boca Raton, Florida. Both main buildings are double-Y in plan, with narrow wings which allow light in every office. The buildings rest on tree-shaped columns which raise them completely off the ground. For both buildings Breuer used a precast window unit which functions as wall, window and sunshade, a unit used in many of his later buildings.

De Bijenkorf Department Store, Rotterdam, 1957. Marcel Breuer and A. Elzas. Photograph by Tom Kroeze. There are large windows for the restaurant and the executive offices. Otherwise the Beehive windows are narrow vertical slits. This allows more wall storage space inside.

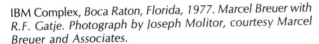

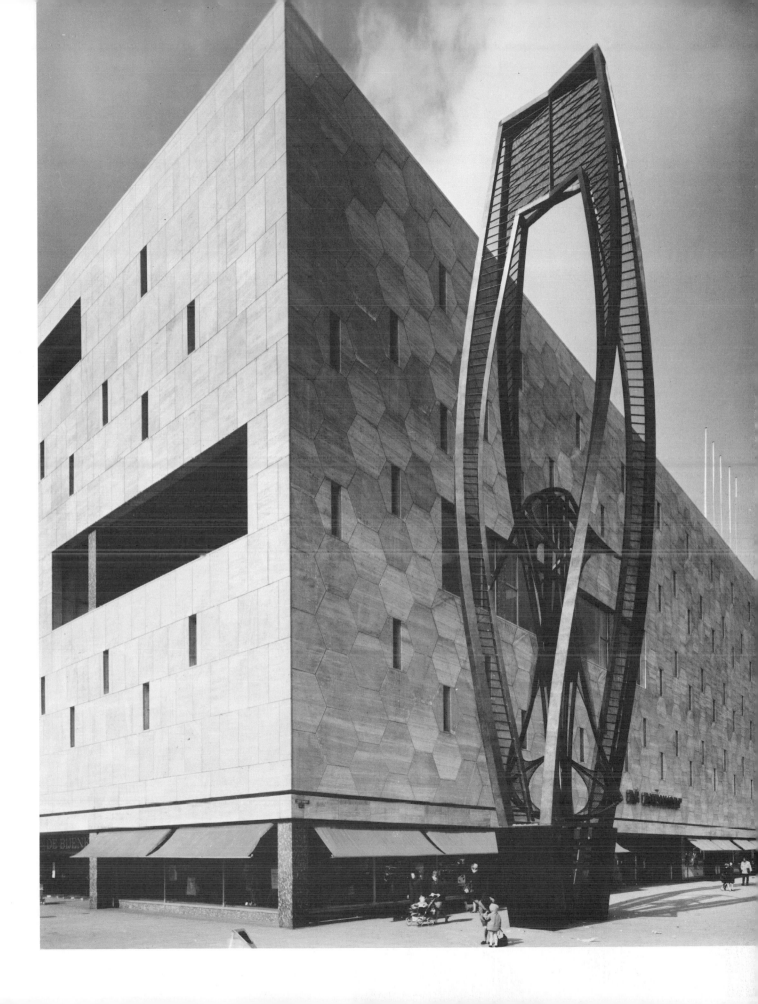

Housing and Urban Development Headquarters, *Washington, D.C., 1963-1968. Marcel Breuer, with H. Beckhard.*

In 1963 Breuer received a commission for a head-quarters building for the Department of Housing and Urban Development in Washington, D.C. The plan is the same one that Breuer used for the IBM Building in France, a double-Y. The HUD Building, however, is wider and higher (ten stories), and only the outer areas of the building rest on the double tapered columns. Window units for the building are almost identical to those used in the French IBM Building.

Breuer and architect Hamilton Smith collaborated in 1963 to design the Whitney Museum of American Art in New York. The Whitney's facade is unusual because each floor is wider than the one below. The first floor, being farthest from the street, provides light and space for a sunken sculpture court. A small bridge crosses the sculpture court from the sidewalk to the main entrance. Inside, the three top floors provide large open gallery spaces for exhibitions.

Street Plaza, Housing and Urban Development Headquarters.

Marcel Breuer lived a long and productive life. He felt that "Buildings should not be moody, but reflect a general, durable quality. Architecture should be anchored in usefulness." His was.

Whitney Museum of American Art, *New York, 1966. Marcel Breuer with Hamilton Smith. The exterior is sheathed in granite, and the trapezoidal windows, built out from the walls* in the shape of truncated pyramids, are angled to avoid direct sunlight.

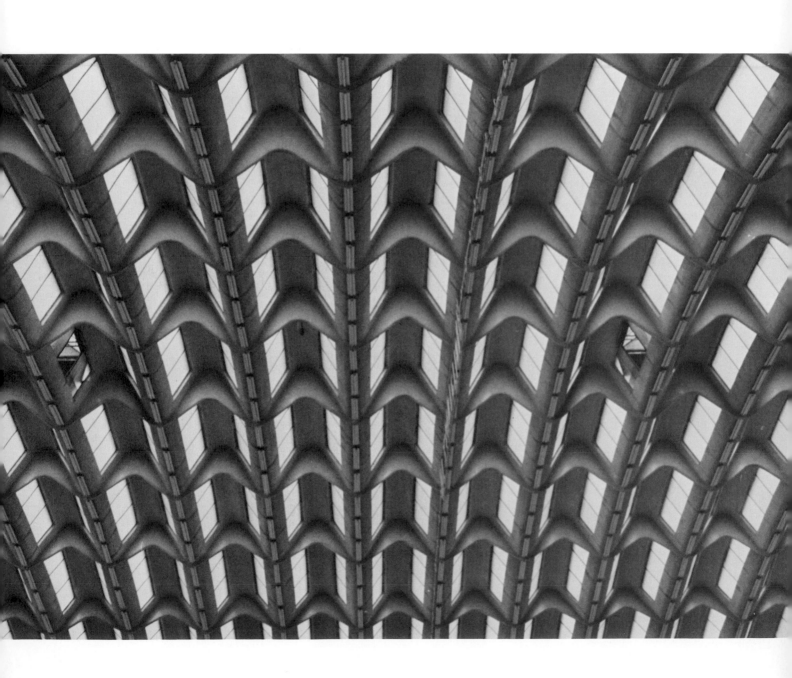

6
ENGINEERS AS ARCHITECTS

All architects must also be engineers to the extent that they must be able to design structures that can be built and used. Some architects, however, place particular emphasis on structural forms in their works, rather than on the seamless integration of form, function and materials. These architects, noted for their engineering ingenuity, are often called architectural engineers. This chapter will examine the works of six twentieth century architectural engineers: Nervi of Italy, Maillart of Switzerland, Torroja of Spain, Candela of Mexico, Fuller of the United States and Otto of Germany.

Pier Luigi Nervi (1891–1979)
Pier Luigi Nervi was born in Italy and studied engineering in Bologna. Upon graduation he worked for the Society for Cement Construction, where he learned the use of reinforced concrete. Nervi's beautifully engineered buildings are notable for their clarity of form and their structural logic. His understanding of the relationship of structure to function was superb.

The first building to bring Nervi attention was the Municipal Stadium in Florence, completed in 1932. Nervi's winning design was chosen largely because of its economy. The structural horizontal beams also form the seats. The roof of the grandstand is a striking cantilever supported by forked columns cast in graceful curves.

In 1932 Nervi formed his own design and construction company in partnership with his cousin. With his own company, Nervi was able to instruct his workmen in how to build according to the complicated Nervi method.

Municipal Stadium, *Florence, Italy, 1932. Pier Luigi Nervi. The exterior stairs are spectacular spirals giving a sculptural effect.*

Agnelli Exhibition Hall, *Turin, Italy, 1950. Pier Luigi Nervi.*

Ceiling, Agnelli Exhibition Hall.

In the mid-forties Nervi invented a new kind of rein-forced concrete, which he called "ferro-cemento," literally "iron cement." It is thin but very strong, exceptionally flexible and somewhat elastic. It is made of several layers of fine steel mesh sprayed with cement mortar. Ferro-cemento is highly resistant to cracking and can be used in very thin slabs and shells.

Nervi's Exposition Building in Turin, completed in 1949, was his first structure using ferro-cemento, and the first to bring him international fame. This hall is one of the most elegant architectural spaces in the world. The lines of force of the corrugated, undulating ceiling are carried to fan-shaped buttresses at each side, and thence to the foundation. For the half-dome at the end of the Turin Hall, Nervi invented a precast unit. These units fill the half-dome space in a kind of double spiral much like the seed-pattern in a sunflower.

Nervi used this concept for a complete dome in a casino in Ostia and for a restaurant roof in Chianciano, and used it most brilliantly in the ceiling of the Small Sports Palace in Rome.

In 1953 Nervi was part of a team chosen to build the UNESCO Building in Paris, with Marcel Breuer and Bernard Zehrfuss. In 1955 he began work in Milan on the Pirelli Building, with architects Gio Ponti and Alberto Roselli. Both of these buildings have much to recommend them, especially the Pirelli, which rises majestically across from the central railroad station.

Pirelli Building, *Milan, Italy, 1958. Pier Luigi Nervi, with Gio Ponti.*

Small Sports Palace, *Rome, 1957. Pier Luigi Nervi, with Annibale Vitellozzi.*

Ceiling, Small Sports Palace.

Three later buildings that brought Nervi world notice were his buildings for the 1960 Olympics in Rome: the Small Sports Palace, the Large Sports Palace, and the Flaminio Stadium. The Small Sports Palace was completed in 1957, with architect Annibale Vitellozzi. The outward thrust of its dome is carried by Y-shaped flying buttresses to an underground tension ring. For the ceiling Nervi used his interwoven panels of ferrocemento in a giant sunflower pattern.

The Large Sports Palace was designed with architect Marcello Piacentini. The exterior is relatively plain, but the interior is impressive. It has a spectacular ceiling dome supported by striking columns in sculptured shapes. Nervi designed the Flaminio Stadium, seating fifty thousand, with his son Antonio. A huge cantilevered canopy shades the grandstand, which in turn covers an Olympic swimming pool.

Olympic Sports Palace, *Rome, 1959. Pier Luigi Nervi, with Marcello Piacentini.*

Palace of Labor,
Turin, Italy, 1961.
Pier Luigi Nervi.

One of Nervi's extraordinary structures was the Palace of Labor, completed in Turin in 1961. In Italy all important buildings tend to be *Palazzi*, and this one is truly palatial. The winner of a competition, Nervi's Palace of Labor is a single large room seven stories high and 555 feet on each side, containing almost eighteen million cubic feet. Sixteen concrete columns support huge flat steel umbrellas. The umbrella plates do not touch each other. They are free-standing and bridged with glass skylights. The columns and plates are the building. The rest is glass.

Nervi's most singular U.S. building is St. Mary's Cathedral in San Francisco, completed in his eightieth year in 1971. It is not entirely his building, though. Nervi was the consulting engineer; Pietro Belluschi the consulting architect; the architects of record were McSweeney, Lee and Ryan.

Balcony floor structure, Palace of Labor. *While under construction, the elegant design of Nervi's reinforced radiating ribs was visible. Today they are obscured with ceiling tile.*

St. Mary's Cathedral, *San Francisco, California, 1971. Pier Luigi Nervi, with Pietro Belluschi and McSweeney, Lee and Ryan. St. Mary's is a striking example of hyperbolic shells* joined to form one of the largest and most imposing churches of the twentieth century.

Robert Maillart (1872–1940)

Robert Maillart was born in Berne, Switzerland. After his studies at the Technical University in Zurich, he became one of the great bridge designers of the twentieth century. He used reinforced concrete in dynamic and elegant forms. He also developed a beamless ceiling system and a system of reinforced concrete floor slabs which he used in designing several large warehouses. He won commissions not because of aesthetic superiority but because of low building cost.

Salginatobel Bridge *near Schiers, Switzerland, 1930. Robert Maillart. The Salgina Bridge in eastern Switzerland is Maillart's finest arch bridge. Because of its isolated location over a remote ravine, its simple beauty is easy to see and appreciate.*

All but a few of Maillart's bridges were built in Switzerland, usually in remote cantons. Maillart's most famous bridge is the Salginatobel Bridge near Schiers. This splendid bridge was completed in 1930, the same year as Le Corbusier's Villa Savoye and Mies' Tugendhat House. In 1930, Maillart also completed the Landquart Bridge in Klosters. This is a stiffened-arch structure built in a curve over the Landquart River. The following year Maillart completed the Hospital Bridge near Adelboden. This was the first of his bridges to cross a river bed at an angle, using two stiffened-arch ribs with staggered abutments.

Landquart Bridge, *Klosters, Switzerland, 1930. Robert Maillart. The vertical slabs supporting the rail line are trapezoids, wide at the base and narrower at the top. This is Maillart's only railway bridge constructed as a stiffened-arch.*

Hospital Bridge *near Adelboden, Switzerland, 1931. Robert Maillart. Because this bridge crosses the river at an angle, the twin arched ribs are set far apart at their abutments. The stiffening slabs join the two arches, creating an unusual pattern when seen from beneath.*

Thur Bridge *near Henau, Switzerland, 1933. Robert Maillart. The Thur Bridge was built of twin box-arches so that the formwork for one could be used for the other. In this bridge Maillart used a pointed arch for the first time. The slab supports nearest the center are less than six inches thick.*

From 1930 to 1940 Maillart built more than thirty-five bridges, some of the most distinctive and dynamic of his career. Two of them were finished in 1933. The Thur Bridge is a low, slim, three-hinged arch crossing the river near Henau. The Schwandbach Bridge near Schwarzenburg is built in plan as a half ellipse. Road traffic flows smoothly from one side of a ravine, curves across the bridge and returns on the opposite side.

Töss Footbridge, *Wülflingen, Switzerland, 1934. Robert Maillart. The footbridge over the River Töss gave Maillart an opportunity to complete a structure using the minimum in material. The stiffening slabs are very thin and the arch itself is only a little over five inches thick. The handrails follow the line of the bridge in a graceful curve.*

Schwandbach Bridge *near Schwarzenburg, Switzerland, 1933. Robert Maillart. The Schwandbach Bridge, set deep into a wooded valley, combines economy with beauty and works exceptionally well. On the outward curve Maillart, with typical economy, has cantilevered a sidewalk.*

The most graceful of all Maillart bridges is a little foot bridge over the Töss River near Winterthur. Built for foot traffic only, the structure is very light and slim, and seems to leap across the river. The construction of Maillart's bridge over the Arve near Geneva is unique. In place of the usual flat slabs the supporting members are X-shaped piers of reinforced concrete.

Arve Bridge *near Geneva, Switzerland, 1936. Robert Maillart. A triple pointed arch of box section allowed the form work to be used three times, resulting in a bridge that was both beautiful and economical. It crosses the Arve River in Vessy, a suburb of Geneva.*

Arve Bridge *near Geneva, Switzerland, 1936. Robert Maillart. The X-shaped supports for the Arve Bridge at Vessy near Geneva use the least material permitted from a safety standpoint. The box construction of the arches is clearly shown.*

When Maillart designed his buildings and his bridges, his paramount concerns were for their efficiency, safety and durability. Each of these aspects had to be balanced against cost: cost of materials, cost of ensuring safety and cost of maintenance. Other engineers have achieved these goals but with mediocre designs. Maillart was a great artist, which, combined with his superb engineering ability, made him unique.

Eduardo Torroja (1899–1961)

Eduardo Torroja was born in Madrid. After his studies in civil engineering, he researched methods of prestressing concrete. When he began work as an engineer, he tried always to fashion his structures as simply and economically as possible. He depended on his intuition to choose a design that would express beauty.

Torroja's first large Spanish commission came in 1933 for a concrete dome for the market hall in Algeciras. Two years later he won a competition for what became his most famous building, the Zarzuela Hippodrome near Madrid.

Market Hall, *Algeciras, Spain, 1933. Eduardo Torroja with Manuel Sanchez Arcas. Photograph courtesy Prof. Juan Murcia Vela, Director, Instituto Eduardo Torroja, Madrid, Spain.*

Zarazuela Racecourse, *Madrid, Spain, 1935. Eduardo Torroja with Carlos Arniches and Martin Dominguez. Photograph courtesy Prof. Juan Murcia Vela. The trackside wall is a series of somewhat conventional Romanesque arches.*

Shell forms, Zarzuela Racecourse. *Photograph courtesy Prof. Juan Murcia Vela. The really splendid features of the stands are the delicate hyperbolic roof shells. These seem to float above the stands. The shells are forty-two feet long but only two inches thick at the free edge. At their thickest they are only five and one-half inches.*

These racetrack buildings consist of two large grandstands and one smaller one. In Torroja's book, *The Structures of Eduardo Torroja,* he tells an interesting story about the genesis of his Hippodrome design: "This design was intended for a competition that had a three-months time limit. A considerable proportion of this time had to be spent in working out preliminary functional problems. But the truth is that the whole process was a matter of a few minutes (possibly seconds), and that these ideas and final form became evident all at once, unexpectedly, at one o'clock in the morning, with only a few days left before the expiration of the final date for submitting the designs and when it seemed certain that we had lost all chance of winning the competition." Of course, he had been thinking about the problem for some time, but his story implies the importance and the force of intuition.

Torroja's next important structure in Madrid was a large fronton or pelota court, where jai alai is played. The structure is a double barrel vault. Long portions of the ceiling are skylights. The lower balcony is hung from the upper one with slender steel hangers, much like the upper balcony in Sullivan's Auditorium Theater.

Frontón Recoletos, Madrid, 1935. Eduardo Torroja with Secundino Zuazo. Photograph courtesy Prof. Juan Murcia Vela.

Bridge over the Esla River near Leon, Spain, 1939. Eduardo Torroja and Martin Gil. Photograph courtesy Prof. Juan Murcia Vela. This steel and concrete bridge has a span of 690 feet—the world's second largest concrete arch—and a crown sixteen-and-a-half stories above the waterline.

In addition to buildings and sports stadia, Torroja designed many aqueducts, viaducts and bridges. Some of his viaducts at University City in Madrid have the lattice-like delicacy of Maillart's bridges. One of his finest bridge constructions is at Esla, Spain.

Instituto Eduardo Torroja (Technical Institute of Construction and Cement) *Madrid, Spain, 1951. Photograph courtesy Prof. Juan Murcia Vela.*

In 1950 Torroja founded the Technical Institute of Construction and Cement at Castillares in Madrid. For it he designed classrooms, laboratories, research areas and a handsome circular dining hall. The school operates today as the Instituto Eduardo Torroja. From a statement by Torroja: "My final aim has always been for the functional, structural and aesthetic aspects of a project to present an integrated whole, both in essence and appearance."

Coal Supply Building, *Instituto Eduardo Torroja. Eduardo Torroja. Torroja designed a three-story-high dodecahedron for a coal bunker for the Technical Institute. This twelve-sided geometric solid is a simple yet singular addition to the main building. Photograph courtesy Prof. Juan Murcia Vela.*

Felix Candela (1910–   )

Felix Candela was born in Madrid, where he studied architecture. During the Spanish Civil War he was interned in France, and sailed to Mexico in 1939. In Mexico he worked in Acapulco and Mexico City, studying shell structures in his spare time.

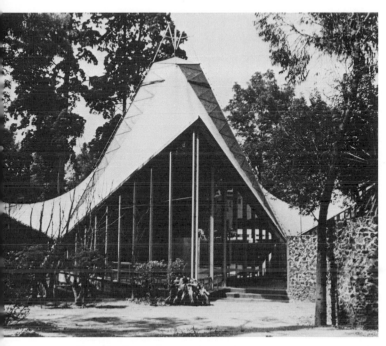

Chapel of St. Vincent de Paul, *Mexico City, 1960. Felix Candela with Enrique de la Mora.*

Restaurant Manantiales, *Xochimilco, Mexico, 1958. Felix Candela with J. Alvarez Ordonez.*

In 1951 Candela was able to build his first publicized shell, the Cosmic Rays Pavilion at the University of Mexico. This small structure brought him international publicity. The Pavilion has a parabolic roof of very thin concrete—thin as one's little finger—so that cosmic rays can penetrate it. To get the roof thin enough, Candela used a corrugated shell. The Pavilion is supported by three parabolic concrete arches of a shallower curve.

In 1952 Candela began experimenting with hyperbolic paraboloid umbrella shapes, "hypars" for short. They proved to be very useful structures, which he employed many times in markets, warehouses and other buildings.

Candela's early shell structures were practical in nature—warehouses, factories, schools—but he came to be known internationally for his churches, beginning with the Church of Our Miraculous Lady, completed in Mexico City in 1955. This is a pure shell structure—four umbrella shapes, tilted and deformed, give the interior a feeling of a most Expressionistic stage setting.

In 1955 Candela also began a series of unusual churches built in collaboration with architects Enrique de la Mora and Fernando Lopez Carmona. These are the chapel of Our Lady of Solitude, known as El Altillo (1955), St. Anthony of the Orchards (1956), St. Joseph the Worker, Monterrey (1959) and St. Vincent de Paul (1960). Candela also worked with de la Mora and Carmona to build the Stock Exchange Hall in Mexico City in 1955.

These were busy years for Candela, who always seemed to be working on several projects at once, but the most elegant of all his buildings was completed in 1958 in Xochimilco, on the south edge of Mexico City. This is the restaurant Los Manantiales—The Springs—designed with architects Joaquin and Fernando Alvarez Ordonez. The most expressive aspect of the Xochimilco restaurant is the thinness of the whole structure, especially the incredibly thin edge of the vaults, the "free edge."

In talking about his discovery of the free edge, Candela said, "Everything is so simple when you know it that you are really angry for not having seen it all at first glance, instead of having to go through the painful process of thinking. I knew the free edge was a practical idea a long time before I understood how it worked and dared to build it." (Quoted from Colin Faber's *Candela: The Shell Builder.*)

A remarkable church by Candela, in collaboration with architects Rosell and Larossa, was completed in 1959 on a hill high above Cuernavaca. Cast in a simple saddle shape, the high edge of the shell shelters the congregation. The low edge is above the altar. There are no walls. A glass partition blocks the fierce breeze such a shape would create.

Open chapel, Lomas de Cuernavaca, Mexico, 1959. Felix Candela with Guillermo Rosell. The Cuernavaca Chapel stands alone on its eminence, the city being ten miles away.

Church of Santa Monica, Mexico City, 1966. Felix Candela. During the sixties Candela designed other graceful churches. Santa Monica and La Florida are among them.

His largest structure was completed for the Mexico City Olympics of 1968, the Olympic Sport Stadium. This huge building seats sixteen thousand. The hypar umbrellas are roofed in sheet copper. When it was new the copper roof gleamed like a giant jewel.

Church of La Florida, *Mexico City. Felix Candela.*

Olympic Sports Palace, *Mexico City, 1968. Felix Candela with E. Castenada and A. Peyri. The roof's main thrusts converge at the corners, and side thrusts go to the tension ring by way of zig-zag flying buttresses.*

R. Buckminster Fuller (1895–1983)

Richard Buckminster Fuller, Jr. was born in Milton, Massachusetts. He was an engineer of extraordinary inventiveness. His most famous discovery was the geodesic dome, which made him famous throughout the world. Applications for the dome have been found from playgrounds to enormous structures covering thousands of square feet.

As a young man, while on active duty in the Navy, he invented a "lightning rescue" device which saved many pilots who crashed at sea. In return he was appointed to Annapolis and graduated Ensign Fuller, U.S.N.

Other Fuller inventions prior to the geodesic dome were an aluminum house; a large egg-shaped, streamlined, three-wheeled car that would seat ten; and a bathroom made of four die-stamped metal sheets. His prototype house built in Wichita, Kansas, in 1944, was a shaped aluminum dome built of aircraft materials. This very successful prototype house was called the "Dymaxion," the name given to his previous inventions—Dymaxion Car, Dymaxion Bathroom, etc.

Fuller suffered many failures—financial and otherwise—until June 29, 1954, when U.S. patent #2,682,235 was issued to him for "Building Construction" which gave him exclusive rights for building with geodesic construction. The invention and patent rights to the geodesic dome meant wealth and international fame for R. Buckminster Fuller.

U.S. Air Force DEW Line Radome, *1954. R. Buckminster Fuller. Photograph courtesy United States Air Force. These plastic domes, fifty-five feet in diameter, could be assembled in fourteen hours and be able to withstand winds of two hundred twenty miles per hour.*

The first commercial order for a Fuller geodesic dome came from the Ford Motor Company in 1952, for a ninety-three-foot aluminum and plastic dome over its Dearborn Rotunda Building in Detroit. Fuller's next important customer was the U.S. Air Force, for radar domes for its Distant Early Warning (DEW) line. The Marine Corps also ordered three hundred domes, to be used from the Antarctic to the equator.

Two Fuller domes made of paper by the Container Corporation won the grand prize at a 1954 exhibition in Milan. Beginning in 1956 the U.S. Department of Commerce began to use Fuller domes to house U.S. exhibits at international trade fairs in Casablanca, Istanbul, Bombay, Tokyo and Moscow.

An early dome by Fuller is the Northland Playhouse on the edge of Detroit. This large, open geodesic framework of metal tubing supports a canvas dome which serves as the actual building. This is not the most permanent of structures, but is relatively inexpensive and provides a large seating area.

Interior, Northland Playhouse, *Detroit, Michigan, 1956. R. Buckminster Fuller. Orange sunlight coming through the canvas illuminates the interior of the Northland Playhouse. The dark seams of the canvas create a striking pattern with the lighter shadows of the metal framework.*

Paperboard Dome, *1954. R. Buckminster Fuller. Photograph courtesy R. Buckminster Fuller.*

Union Tank Car Company Dome, *Wood River, Illinois, 1958. R. Buckminster Fuller. This dome was built from the top down. The uppermost hexagons were put together on top of a giant air bag, which was then inflated enough to add another round of hexagons, and so on.*

Climatron Botanical Garden, *St. Louis, Missouri, 1960. R. Buckminster Fuller. A climate control system allows palms, orchids, bamboo and other disparate plants to grow under the same roof. A double outer structure of steel tubing hexagons gives the necessary rigidity to support the large panes of glass.*

The domes were not only practical and easy to transport and assemble but had great publicity value, advertising American ingenuity and technology. Henry J. Kaiser became a licensee of Fuller in 1957, and produced eight large aluminum domes the first year, including one for his own Hawaiian Village in Honolulu.

Two of the largest clear-span enclosures ever built were the Fuller domes designed for the Union Tank Car Company. The first one, three hundred eighty-four feet in diameter, twelve stories high, and one-eighth inch thick, was built in Baton Rouge, Louisiana in 1958. A similar dome was built the following year in Wood River, Illinois.

An elegant example of a Fuller dome is the all-glass Climatron in St. Louis. Completed in 1960, it is seven stories high and 175 feet in diameter. It has a computer-controlled environment for its plants and flowers.

One of Fuller's most spectacular domes was built for the United States Pavilion at Expo '67 in Montreal. It was twenty stories high and 250 feet in diameter. A Netherlands pavilion designer described it: "It is a masterpiece of technology, and it is beautiful to look at. But it is not designed intentionally to look beautiful—it is a piece of pure technology."

Some of Fuller's later domes were for the United States Research Station in Antarctica, and for a radar dome for a weather station on Mt. Fuji, Japan. There are more than one hundred thousand geodesic domes now, to be found in half the countries of the world.

Richard Buckminster Fuller had more honors heaped upon him than any other contemporary architect or engineer in the world. He taught at dozens of colleges and universities, won gold medals galore, and the list of his honorary doctorates is a page long. This for a man who dropped out of college after less than a year.

United States Pavilion, *Expo '67, Montreal, Canada, 1967. R. Buckminster Fuller. Photographs by Maryalice Nelson.*

Interior, United States Pavilion, Expo '67. Built of steel and Plexiglas, the dome had a system of retractable shading sun screens operated by a computer to work according to the angle of the sun's rays, thus controlling the heat within.

Frei Otto (1925–   )

Frei Otto was born in Siegmar, Germany. As a young man he spent his spare time designing and building model planes. Later he became a glider pilot and learned the effect of aerodynamic forces on thin membranes stretched over light frames. Otto served as a fighter pilot for Germany in World War II, was captured and put in charge of a reconstruction crew in a prison camp at Chartres. On return to Germany in 1946 he studied at the Technical University in Berlin, specializing in structural analysis.

Otto began his professional career by designing a bandstand for a garden exhibition in Kassel. This was the first of many hyperbolic solutions for his lightweight system of minimal structures. Several years later he founded the Development Center for Lightweight Construction in Berlin. His first large scale project was the German Pavilion for Expo '67 in Montreal. This structure gave him valuable experience in creating study models, wind tunnel tests and erection methods.

German Pavilion, *Expo '67, Montreal, 1967. Frei Otto. Photograph courtesy Institute for Lightweight Structures, Stuttgart, West Germany. This structure was based on the tension principle of large canvas tents.*

Interior, German Pavilion, Expo '67, Montreal. Frei Otto. Photograph courtesy Institute of Lightweight Structures, Stuttgart, Germany. Since the plastic skin of the Montreal pavilion was fully translucent, the interior effect was that of a large greenhouse.

Large Stadium, Olympic Buildings, *Munich, Germany, 1972. Frei Otto, with Rolf Gutbrod. Seen from the air, the tent-like cover for the grandstand of the stadium at Munich resembles some transparent undersea creature.*

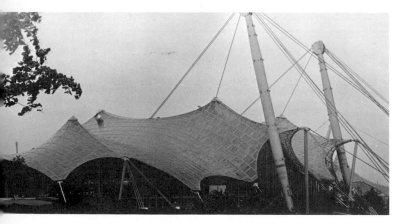

Small Arena, Olympic Buildings, *Munich, Germany, 1972. Frei Otto, with Rolf Gutbrod. The lightweight structure of the small arena at Munich is suspended by exterior tension cables.*

Structural Details, Olympic Buildings, *Munich, Germany, 1972. Frei Otto, with Rolf Gutbrod. Many ingenious solutions were found for the engineering problems arising from the design of the Munich Olympic buildings. The elegant smaller forms which hold the membranes in tension—the hinges, joints, masts, saddles and abutments—are reduced to simple efficient metal forgings that are themselves a kind of sculpture.*

Some of Otto's most dynamic structures were completed in 1972, in association with Rolf Gutbrod, for the Olympic games in Munich. These buildings consist of a huge membrane roof for the large stadium, a smaller building for indoor sports and the Olympic swimming pool building. Connecting these facilities are many handsome hyperbolic membranes which offer shelter to pedestrians. To walk under these floating, weightless, protecting elements on a quiet day gives one a true feeling of fantasy and an appreciation for the creative imagination, the skill and daring which has brought this about.

Frei Otto's latest buildings have been completed in Saudi Arabia, with engineer Sir Ove Arup and Rolf Gutbrod as associates. In 1978 they began building a large hall for the Council of Ministers. In 1981 a large Sports Hall was completed in Jeddah.

Much of Frei Otto's recent interest and research has been concentrated on the analysis of biological structures. He has had this interest for many years. His present role in German architecture is one of mentor and guide in architectural theory.

Sports Hall, Jeddah, Saudi Arabia, 1981. Frei Otto, with Rolf Gutbrod. Photograph courtesy Institute for Lightweight Structures, Stuttgart, Germany. The tent-like structure of the Sports Hall at Jeddah is in keeping with the long Arabian tradition of tents as dwelling places and meeting places.

7

MAJOR ARCHITECTS

Le Corbusier (1887–1965)

Next to Frank Lloyd Wright, Le Corbusier was the most important architect of the twentieth century. He was born Charles Edouard Jeanneret in La Chaux-de-Fonds, Switzerland. When he was thirty-six he adopted the name Le Corbusier, taken from a French ancester. After studying at the School of Art in La Chaux-de-Fonds, he journeyed to Paris in 1908. There he worked for Auguste Perret and learned much about reinforced concrete.

In 1910 he left for Berlin, where he worked with architect Peter Behrens. He learned to appreciate the aesthetics of machine art, of sports cars, ocean liners and airplanes. During the years 1912–1930 Le Corbusier was a painter, a writer and a designer of architectural projects. In 1930 he became a French citizen and began the design of the Villa Savoye.

The Villa Savoye is a white box on stilts. Le Corbusier incorporated into it most of his favorite architectural devices. This design includes a foundation of "pilotis," or stilts, a roof garden and windows in glass strips. The living room is one long space with a free-standing fireplace toward one side and an inner wall completely of glass. A second floor patio is adjacent, open in the center but covered on the opposite side. A ramp gives access to the second floor and a spiral staircase leads to the roof. The roof is meant as a living space, but one must be careful. It has no railing, only a six-inch-high parapet.

Villa Savoye, *Poissy, France, 1931. Le Corbusier. The Villa Savoye is Le Corbusier's outstanding early house. It is comparable in historical importance to Wright's Robie House of 1919 or to Mies' Tugendhat House of 1930.*

Shizuoka Press and Broadcasting Center, *Tokyo, 1967. Kenzo Tange. Photograph courtesy Office of Kenzo Tange, Tokyo. Individual office floors radiate from the circular vertical access shaft of the twenty-story tower.*

While working on the Villa Savoye, Le Corbusier was also designing a large building for the Salvation Army in Paris. This early building features a tall entrance porch glazed with glass block. Inside is a circular reception area. The large dormitory building has windows in long bands. The low walls beneath the windows are painted in red, yellow, blue and white.

Next Le Corbusier designed the Swiss Pavilion, a dormitory for Swiss students at University City in Paris. This was destined to be one of Le Corbusier's most famous buildings. The Swiss Pavilion is a prototype of many of his later and larger structures. It embodies his preferences mentioned earlier: piloti foundations, an all-glass wall, a roof garden and blank end-walls.

Salvation Army Hostel, *Paris, 1933. Le Corbusier.*

Swiss Pavilion, *Cité Universitaire, Paris, 1932. Le Corbusier. The blank end walls are attributed to Le Corbusier's desire to make it possible for his buildings to be placed end to end as in a large housing complex.*

Shortly after the end of World War II, Le Corbusier was given a commission to build the first of his large apartment buildings, the Marseille Block. It was completed in 1952, and is an impressive structure, resting on pilotis two stories high. The Marseille Block is a huge slab twenty stories high, a concrete city with room for almost 340 apartments. Each apartment has two balconies and a two-story living room. The apartments are long but narrow—about twelve by sixty-six feet. The roof garden is large, however, incorporating a gymnasium, a pool, a restaurant and a cinder track one thousand feet long.

Marseille Block, Marseille, France, 1952. Le Corbusier. Photograph by Ruth Barford. Unlike the smoothly surfaced concrete of the Swiss Pavilion, the pilotis of the Marseille Block are left with rough, brutal surfaces, showing every joint and knothole of the form boards.

Le Corbusier had his share of disappointments. In 1927 he and his cousin Pierre failed by one vote to win the competition for the Palace of the League of Nations in Geneva, Switzerland. Twenty years later he was invited to participate in the design of the United Nations Building in New York. Due to arguments, jealousy and bitterness, he left the project and went back to France. However, the basic design of the U.N. Secretariat Building is his.

In 1951 the government of India commissioned Le Corbusier to direct the design and construction of Chandigarh, the new capital city of the Punjab. He brought in his cousin Pierre and British architects Maxwell Fry and Jane Drew to help. The first of Le Corbusier's monumental buildings at Chandigarh was the Courts of Justice, completed in 1956. This is a huge, striking, forceful structure with a vaulted concrete roof umbrella four stories high. Concrete ramps in the unwalled entrance lobby lead to upper floors. A curved concrete grille covers nearly the whole front of the building and serves as a sun break.

Palace of Justice, Chandigarh, India, 1953. Le Corbusier. Photograph courtesy India Government Tourist Office, Chicago. The huge structure of reinforced concrete is topped by a broad roof umbrella which shades and cools the interior. The entrance lobby to the left in the photo has no exterior walls. Here and there, muted primary colors serve as accents to the coarse concrete surface.

Le Corbusier was sixty-seven when his most beautiful building was completed. It is the chapel of Notre Dame du Haut at Ronchamp, high on a hill in the Vosges Mountains in eastern France. Completed in 1953, Ronchamp is both architecture and sculpture. It is one of the extraordinary concepts of modern architecture. It is even more impressive from the inside, with its small panes of clear and colored glass reminding one of a mysterious lighted cave. Ronchamp has three chapels and an outdoor altar, choir loft and pulpit. Inside are hand-carved mahogany pews that seat 200, but as many as ten thousand pilgrims attend outdoor mass on Marian feast days.

Interior, Notre-Dame-du-Haut, *Ronchamp.*

Notre-Dame-du-Haut Chapel, *Ronchamp, France, 1955. Le Corbusier. The south wall has deeply punched windows of different shapes and sizes.*

In 1956 Le Corbusier designed a monastery for the Dominican monks of La Tourette, near Lyons, France. Cast in concrete in the traditional hollow square, the monastery has room for 100 students and teachers. The monks' cells are in double rows at the top of three sides of the building, with the communal spaces for refectory, recreation and library below. In the center, unpaved, is the cloister. The long nave of the church occupies the fourth side.

In 1959 Le Corbusier completed a pavilion or dormitory for Brazilian students at University City in Paris. Designed with architect Lucio Costa of Brazil, this is a rather heavy, awkward-looking building which suffers in comparison with the grace and elegance of the nearby Swiss Pavilion developed thirty years earlier.

Le Corbusier's only building in the United States—his last major building—is the Visual Arts Center of Harvard University. Completed in 1964, the building is guitar-shaped in plan, with a walkway curving through the middle of the building.

Le Corbusier's life was one of economic stability, marital tranquility and architectural revolution. Although he loved the Parthenon, he was in revolt against "enslavement to the past." The chapel at Ronchamp is so beautiful that it alone would assure Le Corbusier a place in architectural history.

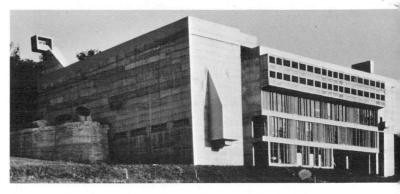

Convent of La Tourette *near Lyons, France, 1959. Le Corbusier. Completely different from Ronchamp, La Tourette has an austere but pleasing rectangular symmetry.*

Brazilian Pavilion, *Cité Universitaire, Paris, 1959. Le Corbusier.*

Carpenter Center for the Visual Arts, *Harvard University, Cambridge, Massachusetts, 1964. Le Corbusier (supervised by J.L. Sert). The facade has deeply-recessed windows and bears strong resemblance to many of his buildings in India.*

Alvar Aalto (1898–1976)

Alvar Aalto, born in Finland, married Aino Marsio, herself an architect, who became his collaborator. An important early commission was the design of the offices and plant for the *Turun Sanomat* newspaper in Turku, a port city on the west coast of Finland. For the street facade of this building, Aalto placed the windows in horizontal bands alternating with light stucco walls, giving the effect of zebra stripes. A huge window reaches from the sidewalk to the top of the second floor, and lights up the left end of the building. The rest of the street floor is glass.

It is usual in Finland for competitions to be held for the design of public buildings. In 1929 Aalto won the competition for the Paimio Tuberculosis Sanitarium near Turku. The windows in the ward block are almost identical to those of the Sanomat building. At one end there are cantilevered balconies on the side and deep-set porches on the end. An open roof terrace runs the full length of the ward block. The entrance foyer is small but gracefully designed and the dining room is flooded with light from double-story windows.

A second competition won by Aalto was for a municipal library in Viipuri, in an area later taken by Russia in 1941. This library, destroyed during World War II, had a straightforward box-like interior relieved by an end wall made completely of glass. The entire reading room and reference room were lighted by fifty-seven round skylights. When plans and photographs of the Paimio Sanitarium and the Viipuri Library were published, Aalto became internationally known.

Aalto's next important commission was a summer home for Mairea Gullichson, heiress and executive of the largest timber and paper empire in Finland. It was an ideal commission, with no monetary restrictions. Consequently, the Villa Mairea is an elaborate, elegant and expensive building, complete with sod-covered sauna, kidney-shaped swimming pool, sculptured fireplace, parquet dance floor and a separate painting studio. Based on an L-shape, the dining and living rooms face a sheltered garden court.

Turun Sanomat Newspaper Offices, *Turku, Finland, 1930. Alvar Aalto. Photograph courtesy Museum of Finnish Architecture, Helsinki.*

Paimio Sanatorium, Paimio, Finland, 1933. Alvar Aalto. Photograph courtesy Museum of Finnish Architecture, Helsinki. This first large building by Aalto, with its strip windows and flat white walls, resembles in some ways the Bauhaus buildings of 1926 by Walter Gropius.

Lecture Hall, Viipuri Library, *Viipuri, Finland, 1935. Alvar Aalto. Photograph courtesy Museum of Finnish Architecture, Helsinki. The ceiling of the lecture room had an undulating surface of narrow strips of wood, a wavy surface that improved the acoustics.*

Villa Mairea, *Noormarkku, Finland, 1939. Alvar Aalto. Photograph courtesy Museum of Finnish Architecture, Helsinki. The exterior is finished in brick, stone, wood siding and bamboo.*

Main Building, Institute of Technology, *Otaniemi, Finland,
1964. Alvar Aalto. Photograph courtesy Museum of Finnish
Architecture, Helsinki.*

Neue Vahr Apartments, *Bremen, Germany, 1962. Alvar
Aalto. Photograph courtesy Museum of Finnish Architecture,
Helsinki.*

In 1955 one of Finland's largest labor unions had Aalto
design its cultural center in Helsinki. The House of
Culture is shaped like a huge scallop shell, with the
stage of the concert hall at the focal center and the seats
radiating to the outer edge. There are sharp curves on
some of the outer walls. For this reason, Aalto specified
that the exterior warm red brick be specially manufactured in a square shape. The roof is of dark copper.

Aalto also designed the Institute of Technology in
Otaniemi, located on a forested site in suburban
Helsinki. The main architectural interest at the Institute
is the large auditorium. Its exterior shape is an obtuse
triangle of 105 degrees. The walls lighting the
auditorium are in a series of steps, the whole inner curving wall tapered like a funnel. Large curved baffles
above the windows soften and diffuse the light.

A German commission for Aalto was for a high-rise
apartment building in Bremen. Standing in the center
of a new suburb, it is twenty-two stories high. It is flat
on one side, at the stairwells and elevators. The other

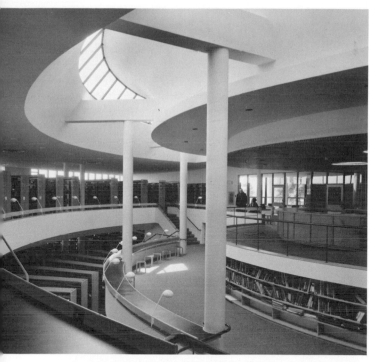

Library interior, Mount Angel Benedictine College, Mount Angel, Oregon, 1970. Alvar Aalto. Photograph by William H. Grand, courtesy Rev. Martin Pollard, O.S.B. The bookshelves on each floor radiate from a fixed point on the inner side of the building. Skylights in curved strips bring natural light to the reading galleries.

Louis I. Kahn (1901–1974)

Louis Isidore Kahn was born in Estonia and came to Philadelphia with his family when he was four. After high school he studied architecture at the University of Pennsylvania. For many years he worked with other architects, then became a professor at Yale and later at the University of Pennsylvania. Kahn's work as an architect became known later in his life.

Kahn's first large building was the Yale University Art Gallery in New Haven, Connecticut, completed in 1953, in association with Douglas Orr. Kahn conceived the building as a simple loft space, with stairways, utilities and elevators housed in a central core.

Yale Art Gallery, Yale University, New Haven, Connecticut, 1953. Louis I. Kahn with Douglas Orr. Photograph by Norman McGrath. There is a certain Miesian quality to the rectangular, glass-and-brick exterior, balanced by the enormous span of the interior, with its tetrahedral ceiling.

side is fan-shaped. This gives every apartment a broad window area. Each window opens to a loggia. On the roof is a terrace.

Aalto's last building in the United States is a library for Mount Angel (Oregon) Benedictine College. Aalto again designed a fan-shaped building, this time to fit the curving, sloping site. The upper floor exteriors are clad in yellow brick and are slightly cantilevered over the dark-painted basement area of framed concrete.

Aalto was a talented and successful furniture designer as well as an architect. In place of the chromed metal preferred by Mies and Breuer, his chairs were of bent plywood. His Paimio chair and his cantilevered chair were manufactured for over forty years. He also designed glass and textiles.

Theater, Yale University Art Gallery. *Photograph by Norman McGrath.*

A.N. Richards Medical Research Building, *University of Pennsylvania, Philadelphia, 1964. Louis I. Kahn. Photograph by Lawrence S. Williams. The airstacks and stairway towers give a strong columnar effect.*

One of Kahn's finest buildings is the A.N. Richards Medical Research Building at the University of Pennsylvania, completed in 1961, with August Komendant as structural engineer. The stairway towers on the building's periphery are reminiscent of S. Gimignano near Siena, Italy, known to be one of Kahn's favorite places. Between the supporting columns run massive concrete beams, clearly visible from the exterior.

Salk Institute for Biological Studies, *La Jolla, California, 1965. Louis I. Kahn. Photograph courtesy Salk Institute, La Jolla.*

Performing Arts Center, *Fort Wayne, Indiana, 1974. Louis I. Kahn. Photograph courtesy Performing Arts Center, Fort Wayne.*

When Dr. Jonas Salk saw the Richards Laboratories, he asked Kahn to design the Salk Institute for Biological Studies at La Jolla, California. In this building the air-ducts are turned horizontally to fit within the box girders. The folded plate walls are faced with yellow-brown Texas sandstone and feature handsome loggias to shade the California sun.

Kahn's only theatre is the Community Center for the Performing Arts in Fort Wayne, Indiana. Here he conceived the stage and auditorium as "The Violin." The lobby and surrounding areas are of masonry construction.

Gallery, Performing Arts Center, Fort Wayne. Photograph courtesy Performing Arts Center, Fort Wayne.

National Assembly Building, *Banglanagar, Dacca, Bangla-desh, 1974. Louis I. Kahn. Photograph courtesy Ministry of Foreign Affairs, Government of Bangladesh.*

Kimbell Art Museum, *Fort Worth, Texas, 1972. Louis I. Kahn, with Preston M. Gerne and Associates. Photograph courtesy Kimbell Art Museum.*

In 1962 Kahn designed a complex of buildings for Dacca, the capital of Bangladesh. Some are square, some are semi-circular, clustered around a central core that houses the assembly chamber.

One of Kahn's late buildings, completed in 1972, is the Kimbell Art Museum in Fort Worth, Texas. The Kimbell is a low structure made of six galleries with varied lengths. All have barrel-vault roofs. At the apex of each is a skylight. The entering light is bounced from aluminum reflectors to the concave surface of the ceilings, giving the effect Kahn wanted, a kind of "silver" light.

Kahn also designed the Library and Dining Hall of Philip Exeter Academy. This building is almost a cube with diagonal corners. The exterior is of brick and purely rectangular. Small reading rooms are on the periphery of the building. In the exact center is a large entrance hall rising to the full height of the building. Opening the walls of the large central hall are four circular Kahn cutouts, each thirty feet in diameter.

Library, *Phillips Exeter Academy, Exeter, New Hampshire, 1972. Photograph courtesy Phillips Exeter Academy. These circular cutouts have almost become a Kahn trademark. They give a spectacular Piranesi-like quality to the central hall.*

Richard Neutra (1892–1970)

Richard Neutra was born in Vienna. He first worked in Germany, but then moved to the United States. In Chicago he met Louis Sullivan and Frank Lloyd Wright. After some months at Taliesin with Wright, he moved to Los Angeles. Here he matured as an architect, known for his use of glass, natural materials, reflecting pools and clean lines.

Richard Neutra's first American commission was for Lovell House, completed in Los Angeles in 1929. Lovell House is built on a hill, and is based on an open steel skeleton built in sections which were trucked to the site. The whole framework was erected in less than two days. The facade is chiefly glass, with white-painted balconies that look as if they were cantilevered but are actually suspended by steel cables. With the publicity for this building, Neutra went on to establish an international reputation. He built larger and more elaborate residences, yet in many ways Lovell House remains his best-known work.

Lovell House, *Los Angeles, 1929. Richard Neutra. Lovell House, for Neutra, compares to Le Corbusier's Villa Savoye, to Mies' Tugendhat House and Wright's Kaufmann House, yet it preceded them all.*

V.D.L. Research House, *Silverlake, Los Angeles, 1933, rebuilt 1964. Richard Neutra. When the house was rebuilt in 1964, after a fire which nearly destroyed it, it was shaded by tall vertical aluminum louvers which acted in lieu of the fire-destroyed shade trees.*

Kaufmann House, *Palm Springs, California, 1946. Richard Neutra. Photograph by Julius Shulman, Los Angeles. The multi-level roofs appear as floating horizontal planes.*

In 1930 Neutra was given some money by a Dutch industrialist to build a research house. It is on the edge of Silver Lake in Los Angeles. This house is called the V.D.L. Research House after his patron, Mr. Van Der Leeuw. It is built on a narrow lot, only sixty by seventy feet, and was kept to a modest budget. It has a standard wood frame built on cast concrete floor joists that span large areas.

In 1945 Neutra completed a desert house in California for Edgar Kaufmann, who had had Frank Lloyd Wright build his eastern home near Bear Run, Pennsylvania. The walls of the desert Kaufmann House are largely of glass. Artfully placed boulders and a huge stone fireplace help tie it in to the desert.

One of Neutra's finest residences is the Tremaine House, completed in Santa Barbara in 1948. Here the walls are of glass. Slender steel posts almost invisibly support the window headers. Whole walls slide aside to create a wide opening to the terrace, a pleasure permitted by the California climate. Cantilevered beams carry the thin flat roof, which hovers over the inner and outer spaces.

Tremaine House, *Santa Barbara, California, 1948. Richard Neutra. Photograph by Julius Shulman, Los Angeles. The Tremaine House has overtones of Mies' Barcelona Pavilion, as indeed do many of Neutra's houses.*

Moore House, *Ojai, California, 1952. Richard Neutra. Photograph by Julius Shulman, Los Angeles. From some viewpoints, the Moore House seems to be afloat in the center of a pond.*

The Moore House, built in California's Ojai Valley in 1952, is a small, flat-roofed residence with large areas of glass. The floors are just above the pond level. Its rigid angularity is softened by reeds, rushes, cactus and evergreens, planted strategically against the lower part of the walls.

During the last ten years of his life, Neutra worked with his son, architect Dion Neutra, to build more than thirty superb residences. These luxurious structures were built in California, Pennsylvania, Germany and Switzerland.

The most spectacular of the late Swiss houses is the Reutsch House near Wenger, Switzerland. It faces the snowfield of the Jungfrau, and the view is wonderful. Glass, with huge sliding doors, forms the whole wall facing the mountain.

Neutra also used a device which he employed so often it became a kind of trademark: the outrigger. In the Reutsch house, the horizontal girders of the ceiling are carried four to six feet outward beyond the wall. From their tips, slender steel pipes drop to the terrace.

Reutsch House, *Wengen, Switzerland, 1967. Richard Neutra. Photograph by Hesse, Berne, Switzerland. An ingenious Neutra invention also used in the Reutsch House, is the water-strip. This is a three-foot-wide pool that is only a few inches deep. It runs along the front of the house and reflects the mountain view. It is not for winter use, but it is very effective in summer.*

Miramar Chapel, *La Jolla, California, 1957. Richard Neutra, with Robert E. Alexander. Photograph by Julius Shulman, Los Angeles. In 1949 Neutra began a partnership with architect Robert E. Alexander. Together they built numerous schools and churches. One of the most striking of their churches is the Miramar Chapel. A spectacular aspect of the chapel is the suspended exterior stairway reflected in the pool.*

School of Art and Architecture, *Yale University, New Haven, Connecticut, 1958. Paul Rudolph. For the surface of the exterior Rudolph used a vertically striated concrete, hand-tooled to give what has become the characteristic "Rudolph ribbing." It is a singular and expressive finish for the exterior of his buildings.*

Rudolph's first large commission was for the Mary Cooper Jewett Art Center at Wellesley College. Richly patterned exterior screens form the outer faces of the main building. Prismatic skylights echo the Tudor details of the nearby buildings.

Mary Cooper Jewett Arts Center, *Wellesley College, Massachusetts, 1955. Paul Rudolph, with Anderson, Beckwith and Haible. Photograph courtesy Jewett Arts Center, Wellesley College.*

Paul Rudolph (1918–)

Paul Rudolph was born in Kentucky, attended Alabama Polytechnic Institute and continued with graduate study at Harvard under Gropius and Breuer. His work is highly personal and easy to identify, especially his larger concrete buildings.

In the fall of 1957 Rudolph was offered the chairmanship of the School of Architecture at Yale University and given a commission to design a new school of art and architecture. Completed in 1964, the school is a blocky, chunky building on York Street in New Haven, with overtones of Wright's Unity Temple and his Larkin Building.

Rudolph designed the Creative Arts Center at Colgate, completed in 1966. The north portico is a huge enclosed bridge. This serves as the equipment storage room. A central light well rises four stories and lights an exhibition hall. Le Corbusier would have liked the rooftop terrace, with its many skylights and access doors.

Charles A. Dana Creative Arts Center, *Colgate University, Hamilton, New York, 1963. Paul Rudolph. Photograph by Dick Broussard, courtesy Colgate University. The striking exterior features strong cantilevers at each end of the western side.*

Arts and Humanities Building, *Southeastern Massachusetts University, North Dartmouth, 1963. Paul Rudolph, with Desmond and Lord. Photograph courtesy Southeastern Massachusetts University.*

The Arts and Humanities Building at Southeastern Massachusetts University also completed in 1966, bears structural resemblance to Rudolph's Art and Architecture Building at Yale, but has much bolder cantilevers. In his Yale building, most of the angles are rectilinear. Obtuse angles prevail in the Arts and Humanities Building. One of the most engaging and most colorful interior spaces is the multi-storied student lounge, with cantilevered balconies above it.

The Christian Science Student Center at the University of Illinois is a relatively small building located on a busy corner. The interior and exterior surfaces are of Rudolph's striated concrete. The building has considerable charm, especially on the interior, with its glowing colors. The neutral beige of the interior striated concrete serves as a background for the striking color combination of orange, magenta and red.

Christian Science Center, *University of Illinois, Urbana, Illinois, 1962. Paul Rudolph, with Smith, Seaton and Olach. To shut out the din of traffic, the center is built like a fortress, with tall, narrow second-story windows lighting the interior.*

Interdenominational Chapel, *Tuskegee Institute, Alabama, 1960. Paul Rudolph, with Fry and Welch. Photograph courtesy Tuskegee Institute.*

Government Service Center, *Boston, Massachusetts, 1963. Paul Rudolph, with Desmond and Lord, M.A. Dryer, and Pederson and Tilney. Several tall towers, curled like cinnamon sticks, bring stairs to the roof.*

One of the most impressive of Rudolph's college buildings is the Interdenominational Chapel for Tuskegee Institute at Tuskegee, Alabama, completed in 1969. The ceiling of the chapel is enormously high, lending an immediate feeling of space and serenity. The russet, red and orange brick and the vermilion seats in the choir provide a welcome warmth to the interior.

A large and important commission for Rudolph was the Government Service Center in Boston. He undertook this in 1962 in association with Desmond and Lord, Pedersen and Tilney, and M.A. Dyer. Completed in 1971, the Service Center is a huge structure built in the form of an angular spiral. On the outer walls tall thin piers with rounded edges support cantilevered office spaces. Rounded forms are plentiful at the corners and on the roof, enclosing service areas. The floors facing the inner court are broadly stepped, resulting in a series of long terraces.

Entrance, Government Service Center, *Boston. Paul Rudolph. Most of the surfaces inside and out are of Rudolph's striated concrete.*

Paul Rudolph has completed a remarkable number of buildings since the mid-sixties, not only in the United States but in Japan and Spain as well. He has won many awards, including the Gold Medal for the Building Arts Exhibition, honor awards from the American Institute of Architects, and many honorary doctorates.

Philip Johnson House, *New Canaan, Connecticut, 1949. Philip Johnson. The steel structure of the Johnson House is painted black, and the house is set almost flat on the ground.*

Philip Johnson (1906–   )

Philip Johnson was born in Cleveland, Ohio. After graduation from Harvard, his early career was in the Department of Architecture at the Museum of Modern Art in New York. Further study led to a degree in architecture. His long architectural career included association with Mies van der Rohe and John Burgee. A spectacular series of recent buildings has led to a new approach to skyscraper design.

Johnson's first important building design was his own Glass House at New Canaan, Connecticut, completed in 1949. The idea of glass architecture had been developed by Bruno Taut in the 1920's, and Mies had already made the drawings for his famous Farnsworth House.

In 1950 Johnson was asked to design an annex to the Museum of Modern Art, then came a series of houses in Connecticut. At this point in his career Johnson's dream came true—he was invited by Mies to assist in the design of the Seagram Building, Mies' New York City monument on Park Avenue, completed in 1958.

During the next five years Johnson was involved in designing fine art galleries and museums. But by the end of the sixties two things happened to him—the realization that he was sixty-five and had nothing to lose by doing exactly what he wanted, and the formation of a partnership with John Burgee of Chicago. Together they produced some of the most extravagant,

I.D.S. Center, *Minneapolis, 1973. Philip Johnson, with John Burgee and Edward F. Baker Associates. Photograph courtesy Investors Diversified Services, Inc. Four of the eight sides are stepped back to provide visual variety and one hundred twenty-eight corner offices.*

Pennzoil Place, *Houston, Texas, 1976. Philip Johnson, with John Burgee and Wilson, Morris, Crain and Anderson. In his later years architect Philip Johnson has become bolder. In his handsome Pennzoil Building, he has defied the conventional topping of a building with horizontals, and has instead used striking diagonals. It is still one of the most distinctive buildings in Houston, due primarily to its simple, block-like structure and plane surfaces, and, of course, its angular tops.*

imaginative, romantic and criticized work of the seventies. Johnson and Burgee completed twenty-five works during the seventies.

One of these is a tall, mirror-finished skyscraper for Investors Diversified Services, completed in Minneapolis in 1973. The tallest building in town, it is octagonal rather than rectangular. Growing out of the base is the Crystal Court, a gallery of glass and metal that is an atrium, a shopping center, a market and a gathering place.

One of the most publicized of the Johnson-Burgee buildings of the seventies is Pennzoil Place, completed in Houston in 1976. Pennzoil Place is laid out in a perfect square, with two buildings ten feet apart in the center. The end of each building is cut off at a forty-five degree angle, and the tops are sliced down at the same angle. Connecting the towers at street level are two slanted eight-story-high triangles of glass, forming a climate-controlled galleria between the buildings, lushly planted with trees and flowers.

One of Johnson-Burgee's latest and largest buildings was commissioned by evangelist Dr. Robert Schuller of Garden Grove, California, for an all-glass space-age cathedral to accomodate four thousand people. Completed in 1980, it consists of ten thousand panes of glass hung on a giant space frame.

Garden Grove Community Church, *Garden Grove, California. Philip Johnson, with John Burgee. Photograph courtesy Garden Grove Community Church.*

Center for the Arts, *Muhlenberg College, Allentown, Pennsylvania, 1977. Philip Johnson, with John Burgee and Coston, Wallace and Watson. Photograph by Smith-Doney, courtesy Center for the Arts, Muhlenberg College. The stark white walls of the Center for the Arts have black punched windows arranged in an off-beat musical rhythm. Joining the two wings is a high gabled window of clear glass, lighting the spacious lobby.*

Interior, Center for the Arts, Muhlenberg College. Photograph by Richard W. Payne, courtesy Center for the Arts, Muhlenberg College.

Philip Johnson and John Burgee completed many innovative and imaginative buildings in one decade of partnership. Critics may disagree on the aesthetic value of some of them, but no one can deny the boldness of their conception.

Thanks-Giving Square, *Dallas, Texas, 1977. Philip Johnson, with John Burgee. Photograph courtesy Thanks-Giving Square, Dallas, Texas. The shape of this non-denominational white chapel in the center of Dallas is akin to a ziggurat, the temple tower of the ancient Assyrians.*

Spiral ceiling, Thanks-Giving Square. *A continuous spiral of stained glass skylights rises with the wall.*

Eero Saarinen (1910–1961)

Eero Saarinen was born in Finland, the son of Eliel Saarinen, also a famous architect. Eero Saarinen's early designs were for steel and glass. Later he made imaginative use of steel and concrete. Some of the most original buildings in the United States were created by Eero Saarinen in the brief years of his architectural career.

When Eero's father won second prize in the Chicago Tribune Tower competition of 1922, he left Finland and came to the United States. The next year his family joined him. Eero graduated from the architectural program at Yale University in 1934. He worked part time for his father, and worked at Cranbrook Academy near Detroit with a group of people who were to become leading architects and designers—Charles Eames, Florence Knoll, Harry Bertoia and Harry Weese.

In 1948 Eero and his father entered separate designs in the national competition for the Jefferson Memorial in St. Louis. When judging was finished, a mistakenly addressed telegram led the family to believe Eliel had won. Days later they discovered Eero was the winner.

Jefferson National Expansion Memorial "Gateway Arch," *St. Louis, Missouri, 1959–64. Eero Saarinen.*

General Motors Technical Center, *Warren, Michigan, 1948–56. Eero Saarinen, with Smith, Hinchman and Grylls.*

Water Tank, General Motors Technical Center. Eero Saarinen.

Eero's first large architectural commission was the General Motors Technical Center near Detroit, begun in 1951 and completed in 1956. The arrangement of the Technical Center is similar to that of a college campus. The low buildings remind one of Mies' designs. The buildings surround a central lake of twenty-two acres. The side walls of the rectangular buildings are glass and metal and the end walls are of brightly colored glazed bricks. Dominating the lake is a hundred-foot-high lineal fountain and two tall water towers in the shape of flattened spheres.

Following the Technical Center Saarinen designed a chapel and theater for the Massachusetts Institute of Technology (MIT) at Cambridge. The chapel is a small brick building with a cylindrical outer wall and an inner undulating wall.

The auditorium for MIT is a three-sided segment of a sphere—"one-eighth of an orange" is how Saarinen described it. Resting delicately on three points, the roof is a thin concrete shell. The three walls are of glass.

Milwaukee County War Memorial, *Milwaukee, Wisconsin, 1953–57. Eero Saarinen. The Memorial has a monumental dignity and a splendid site high above Lake Michigan.*

During this same period Saarinen designed a new building for the Milwaukee lake front, the Milwaukee County War Memorial. Completed in 1957, it is located at Wisconsin Avenue and the lake front. Three of the four wings are boldly cantilevered above a battered plinth, and rest on tetrahedral columns. Inside the wings is an open court with a small memorial pool and a glass-enclosed staircase.

One of Saarinen's most distinctive buildings is the TWA terminal at Kennedy International Airport. The vaults of the roof are a bit heavy, perhaps, with their thick edges, but the interior clearly shows Saarinen's early sculptural training. Hardly a straight line or square corner exists. Stairs, counters, balconies, even windows, are curved. A critic has said that if it were standing by itself and not crowded in among the other terminals it would have been more successful. Still, it is an exciting, handsome building.

Late in his career, Saarinen designed the Deere and Company Headquarters in Moline, Illinois. The Deere building stretches across a valley and faces a man-made lake, which has been landscaped with willow trees and somehow looks very Japanese. The long, dark brown structure fits the site nobly.

John Deere and Company Administration Center, *Moline, Illinois, 1957–63. Eero Saarinen. An unusual aspect of the Deere building is the facade, made of Cor-Ten, a high-copper-content steel that rusts to a cinnamon brown then, after ten years, stops rusting altogether. Saarinen was the first to use Cor-Ten in an important architectural expression.*

Trans World Airlines Terminal, *Kennedy International Airport, New York, 1956–62. Eero Saarinen. Saarinen designed the TWA terminal hoping to express the drama and excitement of air travel.*

Terminal Building, *Dulles International Airport, Chantilly, Virginia, 1958–63. Eero Saarinen. Altogether the terminal is a remarkably handsome building. Saarinen wrote about it: "I think this airport is the best thing I have ever done. Maybe it will even explain what I believe about architecture." (from Eero Saarinen on His Work).*

Saarinen also designed Dulles International Airport Terminal. The terminal and tower rises from a broad Virginia plain about twenty miles from Washington, D.C. Magnificently engineered by Amman and Whitney, sixteen enormous hook-shaped columns soar upward and outward on each side. Cables stretched between pairs of columns support the cast concrete slabs of the catenary roof. It is one of the largest suspended roofs in the world. The columns have a majestic, almost Parthenon-like quality.

An elegant addition to the terminal is the control tower, which is also a restaurant and observation tower. It is vaguely Japanese in character, with a white base column and black structures above, topped by a white radar sphere.

Saarinen once wrote to a friend: "The only architecture which interests me is architecture as a fine art. I hope that some of my buildings will have lasting truths. I admit frankly I would like a place in architectural history. Whether I do or not and how big a niche depends, in the end, on native talent and one cannot ask for more than one has. But one has to work as hard as one can."

Minoru Yamasaki (1912–1986)

Minoru Yamasaki was born in Seattle, Washington. At an early age he decided to become an architect, and graduated first in his class in architecture from the University of Washington in 1933. In his work he has used stone, steel, brick and concrete to create distinctive buildings. His designs range from small and delicate community structures to massive skyscrapers.

Yamasaki's first major commission was an airport terminal for St. Louis. After visiting many airports and large railway stations, he concluded that the great vaulted space of Grand Central Station in New York offered the best kind of welcoming ambience. He therefore designed the St. Louis Airport as a series of intersecting barrel vaults. As one of the first post-war major airport buildings, the Lambert Field Terminal is a graceful and handsome gateway to the city.

The next major building by Yamasaki was the McGregor Memorial Community Conference Center in Detroit. Completed in 1958, it was the first of many buildings Yamasaki designed for Wayne State University. The building is relatively small but very fine and delicate. The white marble columns, travertine walls, striking skylight and general air of stately simplicity mark it as one of Yamasaki's finest works.

A second Detroit building, completed in 1959, was the Reynolds Metals Building in Southfield. The client asked Yamasaki to dramatize one of its main products, aluminum. Yamasaki surrounded the building with a grille of gold-anodized aluminum, and may have since regretted it, because architects all over the country have copied the idea, usually without distinction. The elegant space-frame skylight above the atrium is also structured in aluminum, as are the ceiling panels of the first floor.

McGregor Memorial Conference Center, *Wayne State University, Detroit, Michigan, 1958. Minoru Yamasaki.*

Interior, McGregor Memorial Conference Center. *Minoru Yamasaki.*

Reynolds Metals Building, *Northland Drive, Detroit, Michigan, 1959. Minoru Yamasaki.*

De Roy Auditorium, *Wayne State University, Detroit. Minoru Yamasaki. Delicate ornamentation on the De Roy Auditorium at Wayne State belies the fact that basically it is a classroom building. Surrounded by a moat, perhaps to keep the students in, it nevertheless has access bridges at each end.*

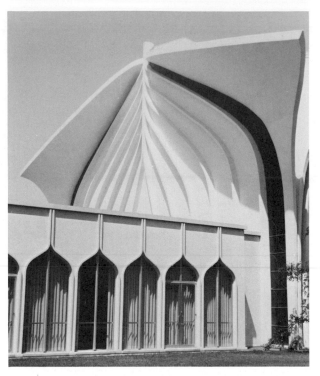

View from the west, North Shore Congregation Israel.

The North Shore Congregation Israel in Glencoe, Illinois, is probably Yamasaki's finest large building. Standing on a magnificent site far above Lake Michigan, it is made of eight pairs of fan vaults which, in effect, form the building. A double skylight between the vaults forms the roof, and precast vertical concrete panels between the vaults, plus amber glass, made the side walls.

Princeton University asked Yamasaki to design the Woodrow Wilson School of Public and International Affairs, completed in 1965. A large pool and fountain face it and create a pleasing and restful ambience. Sixty columns twenty-eight feet high support an upper story of offices surrounding the building. The central lobby is illuminated by a folded-plate glass skylight.

Temple, North Shore Congregation Israel, *Glencoe, Illinois, 1964. Minoru Yamasaki.*

Woodrow Wilson School of Public and International Affairs, *Princeton University, 1965. Minoru Yamasaki. The white stone exterior of the Woodrow Wilson Building at Princeton lends it a pristine Parthenon-like quality. Behind the louvered wall above the columns are offices. The high ceiling of the central foyer is a folded plate glass skylight.*

Kenzo Tange (1913–   )

Kenzo Tange was born in Osaka, Japan. Both his degrees in architecture are from Tokyo University. His first important commission came in 1949, when he won the competition for a peace center in Hiroshima. His museum of the Hiroshima victims stands free of the ground on twenty-foot-high pilotis, and is placed in the center of the site. Its axis is at right angles to the Peace Memorial itself, a small, saddle-shaped sculpture of reinforced concrete.

Hiroshima Peace Museum, *Hiroshima, Japan, 1955. Kenzo Tange. Photograph courtesy office of Kenzo Tange, Tokyo.*

Tange works mostly in concrete for three reasons. Walls of brick and glass are not favored in Japan because of earthquake dangers. Concrete is more economical than steel or stone, and like many other Japanese architects, he is an admirer of the concrete buildings of Le Corbusier.

Tange's two buildings for the city of Imabari are an office block and a civic auditorium. Both are massive concrete structures. The tall side walls of the auditorium building are folded in a manner resembling the walls of Breuer and Nervi's UNESCO conference hall in Paris. Here, though, the folds are wide and deep. They end at the top with broad triangles that support the overhanging roof.

Imabari City Hall, *Ehime Prefecture, Japan, 1958. Kenzo Tange. Photograph courtesy office of Kenzo Tange, Tokyo. The ends of the building are deeply recessed, with a large cantilevered office above the main entrance and a lower block at the street end. The deeply tilted roof overhang at each end reminds one of Ronchamp.*

World Trade Center, *New York, 1974. Minoru Yamasaki, with Emery Roth and Sons. Photograph courtesy Minoru Yamasaki and Associates. The twin white 110-story towers have become landmark features of Lower Manhattan.*

Undoubtedly, the best known of all Yamasaki buildings are those of the World Trade Center in New York, commissioned in 1962 and completed fourteen years later. Wind resistance problems were solved by making the exterior walls into trusses. Alcoa developed a special aluminum alloy for the curtain walls. A five-acre plaza rests between the towers. Yamasaki designed the plaza as an environment for people only, a place to rest and relax away from cars, buses and work.

St. Mary's Cathedral, *Tokyo, 1965. Kenzo Tange. St. Mary's Cathedral is one of the most modern buildings in Tokyo. The textured stainless steel sheathing is an expensive but very elegant and practical solution from a long-range maintenance standpoint. The whole effect as one enters is one of majesty and serenity.*

In 1961 Tange won a competition in Tokyo for a new church to replace St. Mary's Cathedral, which had been destroyed during the war. The new cathedral, finished in 1965, was designed in collaboration with engineer Yoshikatsu Tsuboi. The walls of St. Mary's are in the form of eight hyperbolic shells of uneven size. These rise from ground level to form a skylight shaped like a Roman cross. Where the walls almost join vertically, there are four tall narrow windows of stained glass. The interior walls are of untreated concrete, rather dark and gloomy. The exterior has an elegant outer shell of textured aluminum ribbing.

Tange's largest commission was for the sports arenas for the 1964 Olympic Summer Games. He designed these with the help of engineers Tsuboi and Uichi Inoue. The large stadium is shaped like a modified double tear drop. Its construction is similar to a suspension bridge, with cables stretching at right angles from the two huge main cables to form supports for the steel roof plates. The idea of a suspended membrane roof had been pioneered by Matthew Nowicki in his exhibition hall at Raleigh, North Carolina in 1953. Le Corbusier used it in his Philips Pavilion in Brussels, as did Saarinen at Dulles Airport.

National Gymnasium for Tokyo Olympics, *Tokyo, 1964. Kenzo Tange. The span of Tange's suspended roof is the largest in the world and one of the most spectacular. The sweeping curves of the outer walls are heavy buttresses of concrete, needed to anchor the roof cables.*

The smaller Olympic arena is similar to the large one, but here a single tear drop point leads into the circle. The outer walls are heavy concrete, identical to those of the larger building.

In 1967 Tange completed the Shizuoka Press and Broadcasting Center in Tokyo. Built on a lot of fewer than two thousand square feet, the building developed as a twenty-story tower. One of Tange's largest hotel commissions was for the Akasaka Prince Hotel in Tokyo, completed in 1982. This forty-story building has a V-shaped plan with serrated facades on each side of the wings.

During the last twenty years 1964-1984 Tange has been busy with scores of commissions in Japan and in the Middle East, the Far East, Europe, Africa and the United States. The architectural societies of Great Britain and the United States gave him their gold medals, and he has received dozens of other major awards.

Akasaka Prince Hotel, *Tokyo, 1982. Kenzo Tange. Photograph courtesy Cole and Weber, Seattle. The V-shaped plan provides almost nine hundred corner rooms.*

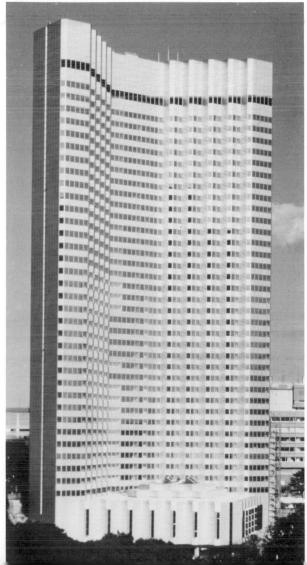

Ieoh Ming Pei (1917–   )

Ieoh Ming Pei was born in China and came to the United States when he was eighteen. He received his B.A. in architecture from MIT and completed his studies at Harvard under Gropius and Breuer. Pei's work as an architect has undergone many changes, from his early office buildings for William Zeckendorf and his Miesian John Hancock Building in Boston, through the blocky Center for Atmospheric Research to the mature and imaginative East Wing of the National Gallery of Art in Washington, D.C. Completed in 1978, this unusual structure is of sharp and soft angles with a massive marble-clad exterior. The exciting interior space is divided into galleries, restaurants and a large atrium with a bridge connecting the upper floors.

National Center for Atmospheric Research, *Boulder, Colorado, 1967. I.M. Pei. Photograph National Center for Atmospheric Research. The structure has a blocky appearance with echoes of Paul Rudolph's early buildings. Set against the Colorado landscape, it has a space age quality.*

John Hancock Building, *Boston, Massachusetts, 1973. I.M. Pei. The tall slim Hancock Building is adjacent to and in strong contrast to Richardson's Trinity Church. The glass skin gave much trouble at first, but this was solved.*

Third Church of Christ Scientist, *Washington, D.C., 1972. I.M. Pei. The simple octagonal form with its carefully crafted concrete exterior creates a sculptural entity. A high triangular loggia is next to the bell-grouping.*

East Wing, National Gallery of Art, *Washington, D.C., 1978. I.M. Pei. The west front with its stark angularity is sharper than a ship's prow. The sleek marble skin burns white against the blue sky.*

The west wing of the Museum of Fine Arts in Boston is a later Pei building. This addition has a barrel-vaulted ceiling of glass running the length of the wing. Pei has also built art centers and museums for Syracuse, Des Moines, Cornell University and the University of Indiana. In his later works he has demonstrated a mastery of conception, for example, his Fragrant Hill Hotel in Beijing (Peking), China, where he has combined traditional Chinese ideas with contemporary architecture.

Recently, Pei was awarded a commission for a new entrance to the Louvre Museum in Paris. His solution is a sixty-foot-high glass pyramid to rise in the center of the Cour Napoleon, the large inner courtyard of the Louvre.

Pei is a Fellow of the American Institute of Architects and received their Gold Medal in 1979. He is also an Honorary Fellow of the Royal Institute of British Architects.

East Wing, National Gallery of Art. *Viewed from the east, the ample windows of the office area are divided by horizontal bands of marble. At the top is a covered balcony.*

John F. Kennedy Library, *Boston, Massachusetts, 1979. I.M. Pei. Photograph courtesy John F. Kennedy Library, Boston. The Kennedy archives building is a simple white shape of pre-cast concrete. Next to it is an eight-story glass pavilion supported by a metal space frame. A broad quay extends to the waters of Dorchester Bay.*

Interior, East Wing, National Gallery of Art. *The interior of Pei's East Wing is a deep and delightfully divided space housing Calder's huge mobile and Joan Miro's tapestry. Balconies, bridges, stairs and escalators are lighted by a space-frame skylight.*

Cesar Pelli (1926–   )

Cesar Pelli was born in Argentina, where he began his education in architecture. When he was twenty-six he emigrated to the United States and studied at the University of Illinois. After completing his master's in architecture, he went to work for Eero Saarinen, whose designs he strongly admired. After ten years with Saarinen, Pelli worked on the west coast several years and founded his own firm in 1977. Cesar Pelli and Associates is based in New Haven, Connecticut.

In the majority of his buildings, the emphasis has been on the "skins," or exteriors. Most of the skins have been of glass—blue, brown, bronze, mirrored, opaque, transparent—with the mullions as small and unobtrusive as possible.

The Century City Medical Plaza, Los Angeles, 1966, is one of Pelli's first "skins." Its four rectangular walls are completely flat and unmodulated, with mullions projecting only slightly.

Pelli's city hall for San Bernardino, California is a dynamic six-story building of reinforced concrete columns and slabs. Its sheer walls are of bronze-tinted glass.

San Bernardino, California City Hall, *1972. Gruen Associates, Cesar Pelli, Design Partner. Photograph by Balthazar Korab. Supported on concrete columns, the western side of the building is raised to provide space for a large exhibit hall. The sheer walls of bronzed glass are beveled at the corners.*

Commons and Courthouse Center, *Columbus, Indiana, 1973. Gruen Associates, Cesar Pelli, Design Partner. Photograph by Balthazar Korab. An enormous interior space is spanned by a truss roof. Part of it is lighted by a shed-roof skylight.*

Winter Garden and Rainbow Center Mall, *Niagara Falls, New York, 1975. Gruen Associates, Cesar Pelli, Design Partner. Photograph by O'Keefe. This tall space-frame building is formed by two adjacent right-triangles of different sizes, touching each other. Roof and walls are both of glass, with red-painted trusses.*

Pacific Design Center, *Los Angeles, California, 1975. Gruen Associates, Cesar Pelli, Design Partner. Photograph by Fred Clarke. A six-story-high galleria runs the length of the building, creating a grand space similar to the great U.S. railroad stations.*

Four Leaf Towers, *Houston, Texas, 1980. Cesar Pelli and Associates. Photograph by Balthazar Korab. The exterior panels have been arranged to avoid the monotony common to most high-rise facades.*

Another glass skin by Pelli is the Columbus, Indiana Commons and Courthouse Center. The faceted bronze glass skin of this central meeting place reflects the adjoining Victorian courthouse.

One of Pelli's most exciting buildings is the Rainbow Center Mall and Winter Garden, completed in 1975 in Niagara Falls, New York. The Garden is especially attractive at night, when the glowing crystalline structure is most visually effective.

The "Blue Whale" is a nickname given to the Pacific Design Center, completed in 1971 while Pelli was working for Gruen Associates. Tall as a fourteen-story building, with a skin of blue glass, it stretches 530 feet and stands in neighborhood of small houses. The nickname is understandable.

One of Cesar Pelli's most interesting projects since he formed his own firm was the commission from the Museum of Modern Art, in its fiftieth anniversary year, to double its gallery space and build a fifty-three-story residential tower directly over the museum itself.

Pelli and Associates' most ambitious project to date is the World Financial Center on the west side of Lower Manhattan in New York. Total area for the project will be seven million square feet.

Addition, Museum of Modern Art, New York. *Cesar Pelli and Associates. Photograph by Kenneth Champlin. The skin of the new building over the Museum of Modern Art has a complex pattern of mullions and eleven shades of spandrel glass.*

Battery Park City Commercial Center, *New York, designed 1981. Cesar Pelli and Associates. Photograph by Kenneth Champlin. This large complex will consist of four office towers, two nine-story octagonal buildings, a landscaped plaza and a winter garden.*

Helmut Jahn (1940–   )

One of the leading young architects of the Chicago School of the 1980's is Helmut Jahn. Born in Nuremburg, Germany, Jahn came to the United States when he was twenty-six. He studied for a year at the Illinois Institute of Technology, then joined C.F. Murphy Associates. Later he became president of Murphy-Jahn.

Many of Jahn's early buildings are in Chicago. The Xerox Center has an all-glass skin with a mirror finish, reflecting what has been called Jahn's "high-tech" approach to architecture. Jahn writes, "High-Tech in its surest sense is inventive, imaginative, with a real concern for function and purpose. It is aided by the latest technology, engineered rather than designed, attending to performance and not just appearance."

Even more high-tech is appearance is Jahn's building at Madison and Wacker in Chicago, the One South Wacker Building. This is a stepped-back building reminiscent of early New York City skyscrapers. Clad in silver and pink reflective glass, it stands out clearly among other new buildings on Wacker Drive.

Xerox Center, *Chicago, Illinois, 1978. Helmut Jahn. Photograph courtesy Murphy-Jahn. The Xerox Center's skin of reflective glass is characteristic of many of Jahn's designs.*

One South Wacker Building, *Chicago, 1978. Helmut Jahn. Photograph courtesy Murphy-Jahn. Pink and silver glass and aluminum mullions form the skin of the One South Wacker Building.*

State of Illinois Building, *Chicago, 1984. Helmut Jahn. The atrium of the State of Illinois Building provides a center for transit and communication, with its balconies, stairs and elevators.*

Board of Trade Addition, *Chicago, 1978. Helmut Jahn. Photograph courtesy Murphy-Jahn. In this addition Jahn has echoed certain features of the original building, such as the vertical window emphasis and the hip roof.*

Jahn has designed an addition to the Board of Trade Building in Chicago. The original rather stately structure was designed by Holabird and Root in 1929. It is one of the early "art-deco" buildings. Jahn has restated some of designer Gilbert Hall's undulating wall strips in the original lobby, using a different but similar design in the entrance to the addition. The exterior of the shorter Jahn building is also similar to the original tower at the end of La Salle Street.

Jahn created a unique approach to a state office building in his design for the State of Illinois Building at Clark and Randolph in Chicago. It resembles a quarter of a circle in plan. Like many other recent buildings, it is a hollow shell. Its soaring cylindrical atrium is topped by a slanting glass roof. Within the atrium are staircases, elevator housings and a series of angled cantilevered balconies.

Houston Tower, *Houston, Texas.* Helmut Jahn. *Photograph courtesy Murphy-Jahn. The pinnacle at the top of the Houston Tower will house a restaurant and observation deck. The building itself is structured in a series of five tapering steps.*

Another Jahn design is for a new skyscraper for Houston, Texas that tapers upward in a series of five steps, each fifteen stories high. They lead to a a a tall pinnacle at the top, shaped like a four-pointed star.

New York City developer Donald Trump owns a hundred acres of land along the Hudson River and has hired Helmut Jahn to design a tower that will be almost one-third of a mile high. It will be twenty-one stories higher than the Sears Tower in Chicago if the city approves the project. Included in the complex will be a thirteen-block-long building. On its roof will be a park of forty acres of grass and trees.

College Life Insurance Company of America Headquarters, *Indianapolis, Indiana, 1967. Kevin Roche John Dinkeloo and Associates. Photograph courtesy Roche Dinkeloo. Structure is of reinforced concrete with flat slab floors and blue glass curtain walls. The two solid walls of each building carry service areas and elevators. Floor space is thus free of obstructions.*

8

PARTNERSHIPS

Some of the most important and distinctive works of architecture in the twentieth century have been planned by partnerships rather than individual architects. In planning large buildings it is almost impossible for a single architect to handle all the drawings. On large projects architects usually work in firms, many of which become partnerships. Noted architect Walter Gropius felt strongly that architects *should* work in partnerships, and helped found The Architects Collaborative In Cambridge, Massachusetts for that purpose.

In an architectural partnership, the work is divided among design partners, engineering partners, interior designers and other specialists. The well-known Chicago firm of Skidmore, Owings and Merrill has nine offices across the country and a staff of over 1,700 professionals, supervised by thirty-six partners. Their services include architecture, engineering, urban planning, environmental and landscape design, transportation planning and interior design.

Several firms usually compete for the commission on large projects. When a firm is awarded a commission, a team consisting of a project partner, a design partner, a project manager, senior designers and technical personnel sees the project through from beginning to end.

Skidmore, Owings and Merrill

Louis Skidmore, Nat Owings and John Merrill formed their partnership in Chicago in 1939. Lever House on Park Avenue in New York is one of the firm's best known early buildings. The unadorned vertical slab surfaced in green glass was a new design concept which set a trend in office building construction.

Office Building, Lever Brothers Company, *New York, 1952. Skidmore, Owings and Merrill. This vertical slab of twenty-one stories is raised above a horizontal block of two stories. The curtain wall of the tower is of dark green spandrel glass and contrasting window glass. The windows are framed in stainless steel.*

Chapel, U.S. Air Force Academy, *Colorado Springs, Colorado, 1962. Skidmore, Owings and Merrill. The chapel is constructed of one hundred interlocking tetrahedrons of tubular steel. On each side seventeen rows of double tetrahedrons sheathed in aluminum rest on concrete posts. The spaces between the supporting members are glazed with stained glass.*

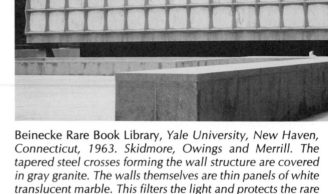

Beinecke Rare Book Library, *Yale University, New Haven, Connecticut, 1963. Skidmore, Owings and Merrill. The tapered steel crosses forming the wall structure are covered in gray granite. The walls themselves are thin panels of white translucent marble. This filters the light and protects the rare books against the sun.*

One of SOM's most publicized buildings is the U.S. Air Force Chapel in Colorado Springs. The startling, sharply pointed A-frame building stands very tall against the mountains in the background.

An unusual building by SOM is the Beinecke Rare Book and Manuscript Library at Yale University in New Haven, Connecticut. Four large corner piers support the horizontal truss frame on which the building rests. There are no glass windows. Light comes in softly through panels of white translucent marble.

Currently one of the firm's best known buildings is the Sears Tower in Chicago. Part of its fame lies in the fact that it is the world's tallest building, ten stories higher than the World Trade Center in New York. The structure of the tower consists of nine framed tubes each seventy-five feet square. The tubes are of differing heights, and are banded together to form one large unit.

Recently, SOM completed buildings in Chicago at 33 West Monroe, at Madison Plaza and at Three First National Plaza. The design of all three buildings incorporates a strong use of the stepped diagonal, either vertically, as in the two plaza buildings, or horizontally, as in 33 West Monroe.

Three First National Plaza, *Chicago, Illinois, 1981. Skidmore, Owings and Merrill. Seen from the roof of the First National Bank the building descends in an impressive perspective of stepped accordion diagonals. The street facade begins with five vertical window bays, then tapers diagonally to the south in a series of larger diagonal bay windows.*

Hellmuth, Obata and Kassabaum

A second major U.S. partnership is the St. Louis firm of George Hellmuth, Gyo Obata and George Kassabaum, founded in 1955. The three original partners all studied architecture at Washington University in St. Louis. One of HOK's early buildings is the McDonnell Planetarium in St. Louis. Its striking tapering spool shape is a landmark in Forest Park.

Gyo Obata is the design partner in HOK. His Benedictine Priory Chapel on the edge of St. Louis has elements of fantasy in its double undulating shell design.

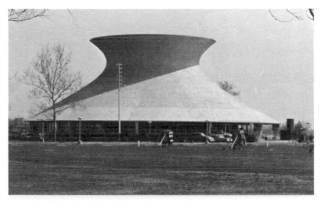

McDonnell Planetarium, *St. Louis, Missouri, 1963. Hellmuth, Obata and Kassabaum. The spool shape of the St. Louis Planetarium is an unusual use of a hyperbolic design. The reverse curve of the upper part serves as a shield against city lights so that astronomers can use their telescopes more effectively. The lower part of the reinforced concrete shell houses a large planetarium.*

Priory Chapel, *St. Louis County, Missouri, 1967. Hellmuth, Obata and Kassabaum. Photograph by George Silk. This fanciful shell design is reminiscent of some of Felix Candela's churches. Thin concrete membranes in two levels form alternating roof and window areas. The bell tower is logical in form but seems to overly stretch the undulating curves.*

Sears Tower, *Chicago, Illinois, 1973. Skidmore, Owings and Merrill. Sears Tower has a structural steel frame which was prefabricated in sections and bolted into place on the site. The tower is clad in black anodized aluminum and bronze-tinted glass. In 1985 a barrel-vaulted entrance galleria of glass and steel was added.*

Interior, Priory Chapel, *St. Louis. Photograph by George Silk. The true nature of the chapel is best seen in the interior. Abundant light is provided by the dozens of large windows with their parabolic contours. A skylight under the bell tower adds more light.*

Galleria II, *Houston, Texas, 1978. Hellmuth, Obata and Kassabaum.*

HOK also constructed two shopping malls in Houston, Galleria I in 1968 and Galleria II in 1978. Galleria II has many elaborate and exciting elements, including an ice rink in the center. Balconies on two levels permit traffic and viewing. A low barrel-vaulted glass roof provides abundant light.

One of the larger HOK projects is a gleaming space-age facility in St. Louis for the McDonnell Douglas Automation Company. It is the world's largest computer center, 810,000 square feet large. Clad in red, white and blue enameled steel panels, the building presents an enormous abstract composition to those driving past it on the highway.

Courtyard, McDonnell Douglas Automation Center. *Photograph by George Silk. The entry courtyard for the automation center offers a change from the flat metal-and-glass facades of the rest of the complex. A series of steps and bridges forms a pleasant park-like area with plantings of shrubs and trees.*

McDonnel Douglas Automation Center, *St. Louis, Missouri, 1981. Hellmuth, Obata and Kassabaum. Photograph by George Silk. The world's largest computer center has a sleek and gleaming exterior appropriate to the character of the company's aircraft products. The strong image also expresses the function of the building as a housing for computers.*

Kevin Roche John Dinkeloo and Associates

Two architect-designers who formerly worked for Eero Saarinen are Kevin Roche and John Dinkeloo. In 1966, they founded, as partners, Kevin Roche John Dinkeloo and Associates in Hamden, Connecticut. Their firm has been responsible for some of the most outstanding architectural designs in the country. One of their first buildings to bring national acclaim is the Ford Foundation Headquarters in New York. The building was made relatively low in order to relate to the lines and planes of existing buildings on nearby streets. Bold corner piers are a dominant aspect.

A larger project for Roche Dinkeloo is the College Life Insurance Company's complex of buildings in Indianapolis. The company planned for nine separate buildings eleven stories high. The first three have been built, and stand as dominant blue pylons on the flat landscape.

Roche and Dinkeloo worked for over a decade on plans and execution of several additions to the Metropolitan Museum of Art in New York. The Robert Lehman Pavilion is a nearly all-glass pyramid which serves appropriately as the key facade facing Central Park. Another of the firm's buildings is the Richardson Merrell Headquarters in Wilton, Connecticut. The building is fitted carefully into a densely wooded area of southwestern Connecticut. The two floors of office space are raised ten feet off the ground on columns.

Ford Foundation Headquarters, *New York, 1963. Kevin Roche John Dinkeloo and Associates. Photograph courtesy Roche Dinkeloo. The spanning beams are of steel and rest on concrete piers. The inner courtyard walls and roof are enclosed with glass. Access to the courtyard park is available from each office via sliding glass doors.*

Robert Lehman Pavilion, *Metropolitan Museum of Art, New York, 1967. Kevin Roche John Dinkeloo and Associates. Photograph courtesy Roche Dinkeloo. The pavilion to house the Lehman Collection is built on the cross axis of the great hall. The central roof is a glass pyramid surrounded on two sides by lower roofs of glass. This allows a maximum penetration of daylight.*

Richardson-Merrell, Inc. Headquarters, *Wilton, Connecticut, 1970. Kevin Roche John Dinkeloo and Associates. Photograph courtesy Roche Dinkeloo. A series of two-story-high balconies allows views of the untouched natural forest which comes to within a few feet of the offices. Both ground level space and roof deck, accessible by ramp, are used for parking.*

C.F. Murphy Associates

One of the larger Chicago-based partnerships is C.F. Murphy Associates, now the firm of Murphy/Jahn. A C.F. Murphy building, the Richard J. Daley Center, completed in 1965, dominates the inner area of Chicago.

Richard J. Daley Center, *Chicago, Illinois, 1965. C.F. Murphy Associates. The building's piers, spandrels and window mullions are of self-weathering Cor-ten steel that over the years has turned a deep cinnamon brown. The windows are of amber glass. Although the building has a Miesian aspect, the self-weathering Cor-ten and the precise geometry give it a character of its own.*

United Nations Plaza Hotel and Office Building, *New York, begun 1979. Kevin Roche John Dinkeloo and Associates. Photograph courtesy Roche Dinkeloo. This first-stage building is a steel frame structure sheathed in green reflecting glass. A sloping setback on the north and a beveled corner on the south relate the structure to the surrounding low buildings.*

A recent building by Roche Dinkeloo is the United Nations Plaza Hotel and Office Building in New York. This glass and steel "greenhouse" structure was erected to provide support services for the United Nations. The upper floors are a hotel, the lower ones are office space.

Another Murphy structure is the R. Crosby Kemper Memorial Arena in Kansas City, Missouri, completed in 1975. This structure has a huge span of 324 feet. It is hung from three giant triangular trusses of tubular steel, cantilevered around the roof edge. These rest at each end on concrete posts. Designer for this building was Helmut Jahn, now president of Murphy/Jahn.

C.F. Murphy's First Bank Center in South Bend, Indiana occupies a whole city block, and includes the bank, a hotel and a retail atrium area. The large space between the bank and hotel is a geometrically interwoven glass-covered plaza. It is glazed with alternating bands of clear and silvered glass. A V-shaped roof connects the two buildings.

R. Crosby Kemper Memorial Arena, *Kansas City, Missouri, 1975. C.F. Murphy Associates. Photograph by Paul Kivett.*

First Source Bank Center, *South Bend, Indiana. C.F. Murphy Associates. Photograph by Mark A. Kelly.*

Interior, First Source Bank Building. C.F. Murphy Associates. Photograph by Mark A. Kelly. The lobby of the bank is triangular in plan, with a butterfly roof that slopes inward. Heavy steel columns support the center beam, and pairs of slender columns reinforce the glass curtain wall. A space-frame of metal tubing supports the glass ceiling panels.

Harry Weese and Associates

The firm of Harry Weese and Associates has been one of the more active designers of distinguished buildings since 1947, with offices in Chicago, Miami and Washington, D.C. A long-term project by Weese and Associates has been the Metro Subway System in Washington, D.C. Its lofty barrel-vaulted stations give an unusual feeling of open space underground.

They also designed the slim triangular Federal Correctional Center in Chicago. The triangular plan accentuates the building's slimness.

Metro Subway System, Washington, D.C., completed 1975. Harry Weese and Associates. In the series of subway stations for Washington, the architect used the central barrel-vault as an effective modern solution for roofing both the station platforms and the tracks.

Two recent Weese designs are the Terman Engineering Center for Stanford University and the headquarters for the Union Underwear Company in Bowling Green, Kentucky. The Terman Center corresponds to the existing Stanford campus buildings with its stained timber framing, stucco-surfaced panels and red-tiled sloping roofs. The Union headquarters building features an exposed heavy timber frame with a mansard-type roof. The interior roof is supported by structural steel "tree" columns specially designed for the building.

A Weese and Associates designed housing complex for the U.S. Embassy was completed in 1983 in Tokyo, Japan. The master plan provided for two townhouse groups of three or four bedroom units and three towers. Facilities include a swimming pool, gymnasium, tennis courts and library.

The partnership approach to architecture is inevitable in this highly computerized age. Residential building aside, large office and factory buildings require thousands of man-hours of drawings. The results of partnership architecture are generally admirable. Partnership salaries can attract top designers, the key personnel in any creative endeavor.

U.S. Courthouse Annex, Chicago, Illinois, 1975. Harry Weese and Associates. Photograph by Hedrich-Blessing, Chicago. The triangular plan of the Federal Correctional Center allows a maximum perimeter space. Each inmate's room can have a five-inch-wide window without bars. Window openings are angled outward to permit a better view. Behind a high wall on the roof is a landscaped exercise yard.

Terman Engineering Center, *Stanford University, Palo Alto, California, 1977. Harry Weese and Associates. Photograph by Bill Hedrich, Hedrich-Blessing. The building is raised above ground to provide for natural ventilation. Above the reinforced concrete ground floor is a deck of heavy timber framing. Glazing consists of floor-to-ceiling French doors which are set back to provide shade and a small balcony for each office.*

Union Underwear Corporate Headquarters, *Bowling Green, Kentucky. Harry Weese and Associates. Photograph by Balthazar Korab. The visitor entrance lobby leads to a two-story atrium with skylights above. Plants and trees surround the ponds and streams. The reception area is a multi-purpose section providing space for product display and a conference room.*

U.S. Embassy Housing, *Tokyo, Japan, 1982. Harry Weese and Associates. Photograph courtesy Harry Weese and Associates. Each tower resident has an individual balcony. At the base of the towers is a landscaped garden with pools and rocks in the Japanese tradition.*

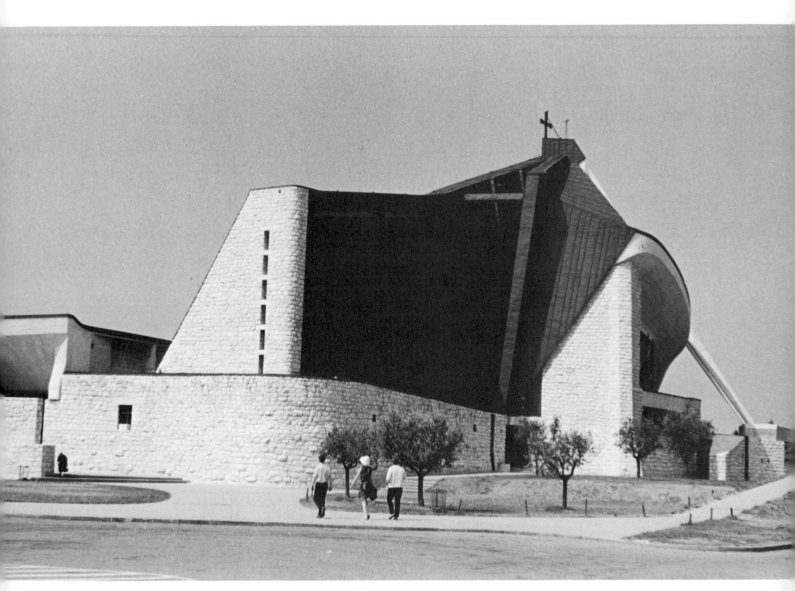

Church of St. John the Baptist, *Autostrada del Sole, Florence, Italy, 1964. Giovanni Michelucci.*

9
NOTABLE BUILDINGS

This chapter includes a few of the more provocative buildings of this century. Some of them have a sober appearance, but many range from the curious to the bizarre.

All except the California buildings were created in the seventeen years between 1960 and 1977. They run the gamut from the striking but serious Museum of Anthropology to the far-out sails of Jørn Utzon's Sydney Opera House.

Opened to great fanfare in 1960, the buildings of Brasilia now seem rather sedate. Arcosanti is still under construction, and will be for decades. Only a few of the buildings are on American sites. The others are in Brazil, Germany, Mexico, Italy, Australia, France, England and Canada—truly an international array of exceptional talents.

Gamble House, Pasadena, California, 1908. Charles Sumner *Greene and Henry Mather Greene. Photograph courtesy Documents Collection, College of Environmental Design, University of California, Berkeley.*

GAMBLE HOUSE, PASADENA, CALIFORNIA, 1908
Charles Sumner Greene and
Henry Mather Greene, architects

The Gamble House has many similarities to Wright's Robie House; they were completed less than a year apart. Both are long, low houses that fit their sites perfectly. Both have deep overhangs, bold cantilevers, roof lines that emphasize the horizontal, and broad bands of casement windows, although the windows on the side of Robie House are actually doors. Robie House is brick-veneered and Gamble House is of wood.

The interior of the Gamble House, particularly the entry hall, stairway and living room, is one of the best of any twentieth-century residence. The Greenes' distinguished use of wood joinery came partly from a study of Japanese timber construction. Many of the wooden posts and beams are hand-carved, and all have been hand-rubbed to a soft patina. The brothers Charles and Henry Greene were architectural partners in Pasadena for twenty-eight years.

FIRST CHURCH OF CHRIST SCIENTIST, BERKELEY, CALIFORNIA, 1910
Bernard R. Maybeck, architect

The First Church of Christ Scientist was built when Bernard Maybeck was forty-eight years old. Maybeck, like his contemporaries Charles and Henry Greene, preferred to work in wood. The First Church of Christ Scientist is a prime example of his skill in using lumber for framing and finishing. Influenced perhaps by Japanese wood architecture, the entire roof framing is exposed, with structural members that decorate the ceiling.

The interior light is moderated by skylights and translucent windows set in stock steel factory sash. In plan the church is a Greek cross. Low-pitched gable roofs are placed one above the other to provide clerestory lighting. Four large hollow concrete piers function as air vents. The piers rise above the roof and are capped with their own small gable roofs.

First Church of Christ Scientist, *Berkeley, California, 1910. Bernard Maybeck. Photograph courtesy Documents Collection, College of Environmental Design, University of California, Berkeley.*

Bavinger House, *Norman, Oklahoma, 1955. Bruce Goff. Photograph by Gene Bavinger.*

BAVINGER HOUSE, NORMAN, OKLAHOMA, 1955
Bruce Goff, architect

Spatial continuity is the most important aspect of the Bavinger House. Yet, because of its design and its setting amidst a heavy growth of vines and trees, it is difficult to photograph.

The house hangs from a fifty-five-foot-high mast made from a pair of deep-well drilling pipes. A helical wall of rough field stone spirals up almost to the top of the mast, enclosing it. Circular pods form the sleeping areas, play areas, Mr. Bavinger's painting studio and most of the other living and storage spaces above the ground floor. These pods are suspended radially from the top of the mast, held by stainless steel cables that were originally biplane braces.

The Bavinger House was designed in 1950 by Bruce Goff. It was built on a minimal budget largely by its owner, Eugene Bavinger, with the help of friends, neighbors and students. It was completed in 1955. Goff thought of it as "a continuing study in contemporary architecture."

BRASILIA, CAPITAL OF BRAZIL, 1956–1978

Oscar Niemeyer and Lucio Costa, architects

Brasilia, the capital city of Brazil, is a large complex of buildings on a wide plain six hundred miles north of Rio de Janeiro. Three important government buildings are built on top of a broad platform. The Senate is in the shape of a half-sphere. The Assembly, or House, is an inverted half-sphere, or cup shape. The twin office buildings are twenty-five-story-high slabs joined by a three-story-high bridge at the eleventh, twelfth and thirteenth stories. The slabs and bridge form an H-shape.

Brasilia's Supreme Court and the Presidential Palace resemble one another. Their broad, flat roofs are supported on the outside by tall parabolic pilotis which come to sharp points as they touch the roof edges.

One of the most striking Brasilia buildings is the Cathedral. It is twelve stories high and has huge parabolic pillars of concrete, yet has the delicate feel of a tiara.

Brasilia: Senate, House and Secretariat, *1957–1979. Oscar Niemeyer and Lucio Costa. Photograph by Luiz Lemos.*

Brasilia: National Cathedral, *1970. Photograph by Luiz Lemos.*

BERLIN PHILHARMONIC HALL, BERLIN GERMANY, 1956–1963

Hans Scharoun, architect

The rather plain exterior of Scharoun's Philharmonic Hall belies the excitement of the interior. This was skillfully designed to give the audience the best seating arrangement for seeing and hearing the Berlin Philharmonic orchestra.

Groups of seats are arranged in more than a dozen sloping areas completely surrounding the stage. The Philharmonic Hall is more than a theater in the round. It is an exciting visual geometry of sloping platforms. It performs practical, aesthetic and acoustic functions, all equally well.

Berlin Philharmonic Hall, *Berlin, Germany, 1956–1963. Hans Scharoun. Photograph courtesy Landesbildstelle, Berlin.*

NATIONAL MUSEUM OF ANTHROPOLOGY, MEXICO CITY, MEXICO, 1964
Pedro Ramirez Vasquez, architect

The Museum of Anthropology in Mexico City is an impressive structure built around an immense inner courtyard. The courtyard's outstanding feature is a square umbrella canopy of aluminum, more than ten thousand square feet in area. Supporting the canopy is a single sculptured column which is also a fountain, cascading water into a pavement grille. The inner spaces of the museum are huge as well, particularly the area which houses the Calendar Stone and other prized archaeological finds.

CHURCH OF THE AUTOSTRADA, FLORENCE, ITALY, 1964
Giovanni Michelucci, architect

Passed by fast-driven cars on their way to Rome or Milan, the Church of St. John the Baptist stands alone in a cloverleaf intersection of the Autostrada (toll-road near Florence). It has no pastor, no congregation. It was built as a memorial to the men who died building the Autostrada, which runs the length of Italy.

National Museum of Anthropology, *Mexico City, Mexico, 1964. Pedro Ramirez Vasquez. Photograph courtesy of Pedro Ramirez Vasquez.*

Interior, Church of St. John The Baptist.

The rough exterior walls of pale, hard stone are laid up in irregular courses, in contrast to the smooth black drape of the copper roof. The interior is unique, resembling no other structure. Slim pillars of reinforced concrete spring from the floor and the edge of the balcony like upthrust spreading fingers.

A critic called the church, ''a raincoat draped on a pile of bones.'' This description is crude, possibly funny, but it poorly describes the elegant interior with its feeling of grace and lightness. Under the catenary roof, the ceiling's smooth curves have been likened to draped silk. All of the interior finish shows the best of Tuscan craftsmanship.

SYDNEY OPERA HOUSE, SYDNEY, AUSTRALIA, 1957–1973
Jørn Utzon, architect, and Sir Ove Arup, engineer

The great shells of the Sydney Opera House rise more than twenty stories above the ground. They serve as the focal point for the whole city of Sydney. The opera house is at the end of Bennelong Point, which juts out into the harbor. The sail-like forms of the shell vaults are one with the sails of the yachts surrounding them.

The vaults cover a concert hall, an opera theater and a large restaurant. All are segments of a sphere, and spring from a high platform. This is reached from the parking lot by an impressive series of seventy-four broad steps.

Sydney Opera House, *Sydney, Australia, 1957–1973. Jørn Utzon, architect, and Sir Ove Arup, engineer (completion by others). Photograph courtesy Australian Information Service. Photograph by Alex Ozolins.*

HISTORY FACULTY BUILDING, CAMBRIDGE UNIVERSITY, CAMBRIDGE, ENGLAND, 1964
James Stirling, architect

The outer four walls and the sloping library roof are made of glass, in the History Faculty Building for Cambridge University. The towers and part of the end walls are of brick. The square tubes of the circulation towers resemble the towers that Louis Kahn designed for the Richards' Medical Research Building.

The History Faculty Building (HFB) is a product of the second stage of Stirling's architectural development. It exhibits a more sculptural and unconventional approach to architecture. The library has an enormous truss roof of steel and glass, which works well, given the number of gray days in Cambridge. The HFB is an L-shaped building, with the library a wedge-shape in the corner of the L. Gallery corridors on each floor are located along the inner walls.

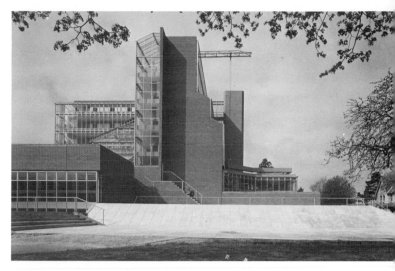

History Faculty Building, *Cambridge University, Cambridge, England, 1964. James Stirling. Photograph by Richard Finzig, Brecht-Einzig Limited.*

COVERED MALL FOR SIMON FRASER UNIVERSITY, VANCOUVER, BRITISH COLUMBIA, 1963
Arthur Erickson, architect, with Geoffrey Massey and Jeffrey Lindsay

Simon Fraser University is at the edge of Vancouver, British Columbia. Erickson's central mall for the university stretches between two low peaks of a low mountain, from the library to the theater. A huge truss supports the space frame roof. Made of wood, steel and glass, the roof measures 300 by 130 feet. The mall is open at each end and covers a series of steps and landings.

Covered Mall for Simon Fraser University, *Vancouver, British Columbia, 1963. Arthur Erickson, with Geoffrey Massey and Jeffrey Lindsay. Photograph courtesy Audio Visual Centre, Simon Fraser University.*

BOSTON CITY HALL, BOSTON, MASSACHUSETTS, 1968
Kallmann, McKinnell & Knowles, architects

Boston City Hall is an outstanding example of bold and imaginative use of concrete in contemporary architecture. The three upper floors are cantilevered slightly, with double piers between the windows. The piers serve as corbels, giving an overall effect of an impressive cornice.

On the east and west sides, tall piers and horizontal beams of concrete divide the lower facades. The general appearance is one of bold virility, tempered by a pleasant diversion of form.

Boston City Hall, *Boston, Massachusetts, 1968. Kallmann, McKinnell and Knowles.*

Arcosanti, *Cordes Junction, Arizona, begun 1970. Paolo Soleri, architect. Photograph by Tomiaki Tamura.*

ARCOSANTI, CORDES JUNCTION, ARIZONA, BEGUN 1970
Paolo Soleri, architect

For more than fifteen years architect Paolo Soleri has been building Arcosanti, a dream city in the Arizona desert north of Scottsdale. The project is only well-begun although it has been in existence for many years. Arcosanti will be pedestrian oriented. It will cover only thirteen acres of the 860-acre site.

Soleri's aim is to create buildings for a city of five thousand people. It may take several more decades to complete construction. The whole project is being built by volunteers, summer student apprentices and some who share Soleri's thinking. So far two large vaults and a workshop block have been completed. Soleri feels that the modern city is inherently destructive, that men and women need to find a new spirituality in a more closely-shared urban life.

Critical Mass Model of Arcosanti, *four by six feet. Paolo Soleri. Photograph by Tomiaka Tomura.*

RENAISSANCE CENTER, DETROIT, MICHIGAN, 1977
John Portman, architect

The Renaissance Center on the river front in Detroit, Michigan, is a building complex created to revitalize the decaying city center of Detroit. The Renaissance Center has four octagonal office buildings, each thirty-nine stories tall with a cylindrical glass elevator shaft. These are arranged symmetrically around a seventy-three-story glass-covered cylinder which is a hotel. All five of the towers rise from a common concrete platform.

The flamboyant effect of Portman's design belies the simple geometry on which it is based. The Renaissance Center (also known as the Ren Cen) is particularly effective when seen from a distance, as an element of the Detroit skyline.

The interior of the Ren Cen Hotel is in standard Portman style. It has a huge atrium space broken by towers and bridges. It is impressive in a World's Fair way, but is no place for those who have a fear of heights or fear of open spaces.

Renaissance Center, *Detroit, Michigan, 1977. John Portman. Photograph courtesy Anthony M. Franco, Inc.*

Centre Pompidou, *Paris. Principal facade.*

CENTRE POMPIDOU (BEAUBORG), PARIS, FRANCE, 1977
Richard Rogers and Renzo Piano, architects, and
Sir Ove Arup, engineer

The Centre Pompidou is one of the most extraordinary and controversial structures of the nineteen-seventies. The building is designed with all the vertical structure on the outside. The east wall is a huge assembly of tubes, pipes and ducts. All of these are painted in bright primary colors, coded for their functions—blue for air conditioning, for example. The effect is that of a factory turned inside-out. It is so startling the building has been described by some critics as looking like a petrochemical complex.

The main trusses are 158 feet long and carry the floors in an uninterrupted span from wall to wall. The west side is nearly all glass. Here there are escalators in a large glass tube rising from the ground to the roof restaurant in a series of five diagonal steps, one for each floor. The Centre Pompidou houses the Museum of Modern Art, a public library, an information center and an industrial design center.

Centre Pompidou (Beauborg) Paris, France, 1977. Northeast corner. Richard Rogers and Renzo Piano, architects, and Sir Ove Arup, engineer.

10

POST-MODERN ARCHITECTURE

Historians are forever trying to separate architecture (and other arts as well) into "movements." Thus we have the Modern Movement, about which most of this book has been written. It began roughly with Louis Sullivan and the Chicago School in the late nineteenth century.

But has it ended? Yes, a long time ago, say some writers, architects and historians. They claim it ended around 1960, but carried over into a sliding decade called "Late Modern." That, according to certain of the *avant-garde*, is now old hat, and the reigning style, though perhaps not the most frequently used, is now something called "Post-Modern."

Why did Post-Modern architecture develop? Probably it is because architects began to realize what the public has known (and shown) for a long time, that it is tired of the plain glass box. Suddenly the Chrysler Building is more interesting and appealing than Lever House or the Seagram Building. The public taste has never really accepted the machine age, even though we all live in it and would be lost without it. Not all Modern architecture is plain glass boxes, of course.

True, there are movements back to country living, to wood stoves, but not often to outhouses or to kerosene lamps. We like our gadgets, our dishwashers, compacters, food processors, hair dryers. But we also like a little bit of decoration, a few curves, a few columns, a few cupolas. It is with good reason that Disneyland and other amusement parks are full of castles and Victorian designs.

Many architects have grown tired of the white rectangular boxes of Gropius and Le Corbusier, of the skin and bones of Mies, and have reverted to a kind of historical nostalgia for columns and capitals, pediments, keystones and cornices. The Getty Museum in Malibu, California, built in 1975, is an exaggerated example of Post-Modern Classicism a recreated Pompeian villa, complete with chlorinated water and a parking garage.

Post-Modern architecture is not fully accepted today, as can be seen in the furor over Michael Graves' design for the Portland Public Office Building in Oregon. Letters to the editor called it funny, a complete joke, archaic, gaudy and offensive. The city council approved it, however, because the design met all the major specifications and was estimated at $61.90 a square foot compared to a competing design at $90.02 a square foot. While the Portland chapter of the AIA (the American Institute of Architects) generally disapproved, the national council of the AIA gave the building one of their eleven honor awards for 1983. Graves disclaims the label "Post-Modernist," although he does lean heavily on historical sources.

According to some experts on Post-Modernism, there are several aspects that help distinguish it from Modern architecture. Among them are layering, metaphor, historical allusion, applied ornament, poetic distortions, ambiguity of space and emphasis on perspective. Curves and arches are used more often. Graphics or supergraphics are often applied, and strong contrasting colors are used. Of course, not all of the above are found in one building.

"Animal Crackers" House at Highland Park, Illinois, 1978. Stanley Tigerman with Robert Fugman. Photograph by Howard N. Kaplan. In this building Tigerman combines the standard vertical wood siding of many conventional houses with the exuberant curves found in several of his other buildings. The reverse curves of the entrance windows with the nose-like lamp above the door caricature the smiling face of an animal.

169

Portland Public Services Building, *Portland, Oregon, 1982. Michael Graves. Photograph courtesy Ackroyd Photography. The Portland Building is the first major public building in the Post-Modern mode. Classical allusions abound, from the colonnade at the base to the pilasters rising to the keystone shape at the top. The color on the exterior are rich and vibrant—pale yellow walls, burnt-sienna keystones and sea green tile on the base. Critics have called it everything from "Pop-Surrealism" to gracious and lively.*

Space in Post-Modern designs often has unclear boundaries. Some architects treat space as an almost-tangible object. A door, for instance, may be created so narrow that one must go through it sideways. *That* makes space almost tangible.

Many Post-Modern architects achieve a layering of space by superimposing a wall or part of a wall in front of another. This may involve a screen or a grille. More often it is by use of a solid, thin wall with openings, cutouts that seldom line up with similar openings in the wall behind. This produces a feeling of ambiguity. During the sixties superimposition was developed. Designers created relationships among layers of space, among objects within objects and rooms within rooms.

Post-Modern space is generally dense and rich, free-form and often skewed, given sharp angles which exaggerate perspective. It is complex, compared with the simplicity of space in Mies van der Rohe's designs.

The use of metaphor is sometimes explicit. Some Post-Modern houses have facades that are made to look like faces, with round windows above and on each side of the central door. In other cases the metaphor is unintentional, as in Pelli's "Blue Whale" (the Pacific Design Center, see p. 145).

Charles Moore

Charles Moore's work pulls together many of the themes of Post-Modernism. He shows us the possiblities and present limits of this approach. One of Moore's most delightful fantasies is the Piazza d'Italia, completed in New Orleans in 1979, with Perez Associates of New Orleans. The Piazza is a group of varied arches using all the old Italian orders in inventive and imaginative ways, some outlined in pink neon.

Piazza d'Italia, *New Orleans, Louisiana, 1979. Charles Moore. Photograph by Wyatt Wade.*

Peter Eisenman

The exteriors of the houses of Peter Eisenman, except for their multi-colors and their accent on layering, are somewhat reminiscent of Gropius and Le Corbusier. Inside them the Post-Modern treatment of space is immediately apparent. In a house for Robert Miller in Lakeville, Connecticut, 1971, bridges and open volumes divide the room functions, and within the apparently square grid of the house is hidden another square house set at forty-five degrees to the outer one, which leads to a real ambiguity of space. This is characteristic of Post-Modern architecture but it is not usually so emphatic.

Carll Tucker II House, *Katonah, New York, 1975. Venturi, Rauch and Scott-Brown. Photograph by Tom Crane. The roof of the Tucker House is a steep pyramid deeply overhanging the facade. The living room is located directly below the roof. A large oval bull's-eye window dominates the main facade and breaks up the internal space. Beneath it is a pair of large windows and below them a band of ribbon windows.*

Venturi, Rauch and Scott Brown

Robert Venturi, John Rauch and Denise Scott Brown have produced some outstanding architectural work in recent years. Venturi has negated Mies' dictum "less is more" by stating "less is a bore" and "more is more."

Venturi incorporates everyday objects such as used furniture, posters, signs and graphics. He favors use of many architectural elements, from classical arches and columns to signs and billboards. One of the best-known of Venturi, Rauch and Scott Brown's works is the house built for Carll Tucker in Katonah, New York in 1975. On the facade, a giant bulls-eye window breaks through the edge of the oversized pediment roof, while below the first floor are traditional banded windows. The same overscaled proportions occur in the interior as well.

Richard Meier

Richard Meier's most notable Post-Modern buildings have been houses, and one of the most publicized is the Smith House in Darien, Connecticut, built in 1967. There is a definite reflection of Le Corbusier in this house. It is white and angular, but there the resemblance ends. The aspect of "layering" is perhaps more noticeable here than in any other Post-Modern designs. The house is sited in deep woods and stands out strongly as a white, man-made element, with many layers of horizontal and vertical walls and screens.

Smith House, *Darien, Connecticut, 1967. Richard Meier. Photograph by Ezra Stoller, courtesy Richard Meier and Associates. The highly reflective surfaces of the ocean side of the Smith House catch light and color from the sea, the sky and the trees. The tall slender chimney of painted brick seems incredibly thin. The large upper windows form the wall of the living room, overlooking Long Island Sound.*

Hartford Seminary Chapel, *Hartford, Connecticut. Richard Meier. Photograph by Ezra Stoller, courtesy Richard Meier and Associates. Like many of Meier's buildings, the Hartford Seminary Chapel has a distinctly cubist aura, as if it might have been a painting by Charles Jeanneret before he became Le Corbusier. The emphasis here is again on all-white block-like forms, articulated with great care and facility. The windows in the main facade are checkerboarded rather than banded, offering a chaste decoration.*

Best Products Facade Project, *1979. Robert A.M. Stern Architects. Model by John Ike and Mark Gilbert. Photograph courtesy Robert A.M. Stern Architects. This proposal for a wayside Best Products catalog showroom is full of metaphors. The sloping pediment frame symbolizes the temple of consumerism, saying that shopping is a cultural act. The main entrance opening and each of the smaller ones is a Greek column in negative. The letter "T" is placed to rest directly over the main entrance. The square spaces (metopes) above each small entrance are cut-out shapes indicating the products within.*

Robert Stern

Robert Stern has designed showrooms, apartments, offices and houses, but is better known as an author and teacher. He feels that eclecticism, the use or influence of earlier styles of architecture, is an advantage, not a crime. He believes in applied ornament as a relief from pure technology.

One of Stern's most interesting recent works is a project for a new tower for the Chicago Tribune. The Tribune project, dated 1980, is based loosely on the 1922 entry by Adolf Loos in the original Chicago Tribune competition. Loos' entry was twenty-two-story-high giant Doric column springing from a twelve-story base, with a square cornice observatory floor at the top of the column. Stern's column is square, and thicker than that of Loos. It rises from a well-proportioned base. It has triple Tuscan red pilasters forming each side. These taper outward at the top to support a large cornice signboard which wraps around all four sides of the building. "Chicago" is written on two opposite sides and "Tribune" on the other two sides.

Chicago Tribune Tower Project, *1980. Robert A.M. Stern Architects. Photograph courtesy Robert A.M. Stern Architects. In this competition design Stern reflects the Greek column of Adolf Loos in the original 1922 competition and combines it with a Miesian squared-off glass facade. On each side rise classical pilasters of red reflecting glass. The corners are of striped black-and-white glass, a metaphor for newsprint.*

Hot Dog House, Harvard, Illinois. Stanley Tigerman. Photograph courtesy Stanley Tigerman. Tigerman's "Hot Dog" house stands atop a hill near Harvard, Illinois. Seen from the air it has the long narrow outline of a hot dog, rounded at each end. Between the cedarwood ends, the lakeside wall is nearly all glass.

Stanley Tigerman

Stanley Tigerman is among Chicago architects who sometimes work in the Post-Modern style. In what he calls his "surreal" houses, Tigerman relies heavily on metaphor. For instance, a house in Harvard, Illinois, with a long, narrow floor plan rounded at each end he calls the "Hot Dog House." It is more like a bratwurst, but the metaphor works. Except for a narrow central doorway, the two-story facade facing the highway is a blank wall of vertical cedar boards. The back side, facing a small lake, is all glass.

A second Tigerman house is called "Animal Crackers." It was completed in Highland Park, Illinois, in 1978, with Robert Fugman as associate. The rounded, curving facade does bear some resemblance to an animal cracker. The architects' intention was to transcend the usual suburban residential pattern.

Other Tigerman buildings based on metaphor are the Daisy House in Porter, Indiana; a large two-car garage in Chicago in the profile of a motor car; and the House with a Pompadour in Ogden Dunes, Indiana in which the facade design was based on the client's hair style.

Austrian Travel Bureau, Vienna, 1978. Hans Hollein. Photograph by Jerzy Surwillo. Hollein's Travel Office in Vienna is an exciting manifestation of his imaginative approach to interior design. It is full of metaphors. The polished brass palm trees suggest trips to southern climes. Rows of fat Doric columns suggest a visit to Athens. The arc of a barrel-vaulted skylight covers all of the main hall. It is intentionally reminiscent of Otto Wagner's Post Office Savings Bank.

Hans Hollein

Hans Hollein is a Viennese architect who has studied and worked in many parts of the world. His 1978 design for the Austrian State Travel Bureau in Vienna is worth noting. Hollein's building incorporates many exotic elements relating to travel fantasies. His shiny brass-columned trees with metal leaves are similar to those in John Nash's Royal Pavilion in Brighton, England. Hollein's Travel Bureau has a brass-domed oriental pavilion which serves as a small, elegant rest area. The Travel Bureau also has a small theater-like desk framed by draped metal curtains. Here theater tickets are sold. Hollein has relied heavily on metaphor for this work, such as relating palm trees to a travel paradise for Austrians.

The general public has finally accepted Modern Art up to 1880, the paintings of the Impressionists and Post-Impressionists. Yet it has never fully accepted Modern architecture for residential use: the flat facades of Le Corbusier and Gropius or the glass boxes of Mies. "We want a little decoration" is almost a universal cry. This cry has been heard, in fact, echoed, by Late-Modern, Post-Modern and Supermannerist architects, and the best of them have answered it with grace and skill.

There also exists the awful probability that some really terrible Post-Modern "architecture" will come to be built. The fact is, of course, that Post-Modernism, like all new movements, will soon become an academy, and Attila and his architect Huns will be waiting in the hills to swoop down and kill it. But this is all to the good. Just think how boring life would be if we were all still living and working in the Roman architecture of the first century A.D.

Interior, Villa Savoye, *Poissy, France, 1931. Le Corbusier.*

GLOSSARY

abutment. A block of concrete or masonry placed to absorb the thrust of a vault, or the thrusts of an arch at each end of a bridge.

acrophobia. Fear of being in high places.

Alhambra. Fourteenth century palace of the Moorish kings in Granada, Spain.

ambience. The particular atmosphere of a certain place, sometimes pleasant, sometimes not.

anodized. Coated electrolytically with a colored oxide, as on aluminum or other metal.

apse. A projection of a building, often the altar area at the east end of a church.

arabesque. A complex design of interwoven floral or geometric figures.

arcade. A series of arches resting on piers or columns. Sometimes a glass-covered passageway with shops on either side.

asymmetric. Not symmetrical, i.e., unevenly divided.

atrium. An open central court, today usually glass-covered. Originally the central court of ancient Roman houses.

baffle. A sheet of building material designed to reduce the effect of light, sound or air currents.

balloon framing. A method of timber framing used particularly in the United States. Two-by-four vertical studs are nailed to horizontal members on sixteen inch centers.

Baroque. A style in 16th and 17th century European art and architecture typified by elaborate and ornate scrolls and curves and complex spatial compositions.

bay. Exterior division of a building marked by vertical window patterns or projections. Usually multiple.

bay window. A large window extending from the outer wall of a building and forming a recess within. If curved, called a bow window.

beam. A horizontal supporting member of wood, metal or reinforced concrete used in construction.

bisymmetrical. Evenly divided into two sides.

board and batten. A wall surface, usually exterior, made up of wide boards, the joints of which are covered with narrow boards (battens).

box girder. A U-shaped concrete beam, as used by Maillart in some of his bridges.

butterfly roof. Opposite to the gable roof, the two slabs of the butterfly roof slope downward to the center, somewhat like the wings of a butterfly at rest.

buttress. A support placed to oppose the outward thrusts of a structure, as in the Gothic flying buttress.

Byzantine. Pertaining to the Byzantine Empire. Byzantine architecture is characterized by masonry construction, round arches and domed roofs.

calligraphy. Decorative handwriting, often with a great many flourishes.

canopy. An overhanging projection, usually stretching from a doorway to the curb.

cantilever. A rigid horizontal construction extending well beyond its vertical support. The wings of an airplane are cantilevered.

catenary. A catena in Latin is a chain, and a catenary is a curve made by a chain or rope hanging from two points some distance from each other.

chamfer. A beveled or slanted area formed at the corner of a board, square post or pier.

clerestory. A wall with windows rising above extended roofs below, bringing daylight into the interior of a building.

cloister. A covered walkway, usually with an arcade or colonnade opening onto a courtyard. Common to monasteries or convents.

coffered. Made with recessed panels, usually square or octagonal, as ornaments for a ceiling or a vault.

corbel. A masonry block projecting from a wall, used to support a beam or vault.

corbeled arch. A kind of arch built up with layers of courses on each side, becoming progressively closer to each other until they meet.

cornice. A projecting continuous horizontal element on the exterior of a building, usually located at or near the top.

corrugated. Formed into a series of furrows and ridges, as in the filler of paper carton board or in metal or plastic roofing sheets.

cruciform. Cross-shaped.

cupola. A light structure on a roof or a dome, often serving as a lantern or observation point.

curtain-wall. A non-loadbearing wall, usually of glass or thin metal, hung on the framing of many modern buildings.

Doric. An early classical order of Greek architecture. Fluted columns without bases rise to simple capitals, each with a square top.

eave. The overhanging lower edge of a roof.

Expressionism. In architecture, a 20th century movement based primarily in Germany, in which a highly imaginative and subjective approach produced few buildings but many dynamic and influential sketches.

facade. A French word meaning front. The front of a building.

fan vault. A vault which spreads out from its base. In English Gothic, a vault in which the ribs spread out from each of the four corners.

fenestration. The design and arrangement of the windows of a building.

finials. Ornamental finishing features at the top of pinnacles or spires.

flying buttress. In Gothic churches, a buttress in the form of an arch that carries the thrust of the nave vault over the side aisles to a massive outer pier.

folded plate. Wall, ceiling or roof structures of various materials, resembling folded paper in design.

folded slab. Similar to folded plate, but broader and heavier in construction.

foundry. A shop where metal is cast.

foyer. A lobby of a theater or hotel; a vestibule or entrance hall of a house.

fronton. A building in which the Spanish game of jai alai is played.

gable. The part of the front or side of a building forming a triangle under a pitched roof.

galleria. Modern variation of a gallery. Usually refers to a large, open, glassed-in space hundreds of square feet in area, housing shops and service establishments.

gallery. A long narrow passageway, usually roofed with glass, open at one or both ends.

gambrel roof. A gable roof with two angles on each side, a shallow one above a steeper one. Many barns have gambrel roofs.

geodesic. Referring to the geometry of curved surfaces. A geodesic dome combines the structural properties of the tetrahedron and the sphere.

girder. A major horizontal supporting beam, usually of steel or reinforced concrete.

glass-butted. Where glass walls are joined at a corner or in-line without the use of metal or wood strips.

Greek cross. A cross in which all the arms are of equal length.

grille. A perforated screen, often decorative, used to cover an area. Used in architecture as a sunscreen or privacy screen.

header. A strong beam above a door or window opening in the framing of a wall.

hypar. Abbreviation for hyperbolic paraboloid.

hyperbolic. Pertaining to or derived from a hyperbola, a conic section.

hyperbolic paraboloid. Basically a saddle shape. When cut in the horizontal plane the curves are hyperbolas. When cut in the vertical plane the curves are parabolas.

I-beam. A beam of steel or concrete shaped like the letter "I" in cross-section.

iconoclastic. Descriptive of breaking or destroying images, or attacking beliefs or traditional institutions.

Impressionism. A style of painting developed in France in the last third of the 19th century. Short brush strokes and bright colors were used to create the impression of light on objects.

International Style. A style of modern architecture developed in the 1920's and 1930's, characterized by simple geometric forms, windows in bands or large masses, and flat, often white exterior walls.

Ionic. A classical order of ancient Greece, with fluted columns on molded bases and capitals with scroll-shaped elements.

Italianate. Influenced by Italian styles or customs.

joist. One of a number of parallel beams of wood, steel or concrete used to support floors or ceilings.

keystone. The wedge-shaped stone at the center of an arch.

lintel. A horizontal beam above an opening in a wall, supporting the weight above it. At Stonehenge, the horizontal members resting on the vertical stones.

loggia. An enclosed area on the side of a building, open to the air on one side. Sometimes open on two sides when placed at the corner of a building.

lunette. A part of a wall area above a door or window, usually semi-circular in outline.

Macassar ebony. A rich black wood from an area in Central Indonesia.

majolica. Pottery or ceramic tiles covered with an opaque glaze, usually highly decorated.

mansard. A four-sided roof with two slopes, the upper one almost flat and the lower one close to the vertical.

masonry. Usually brick or stone work bonded with mortar (cement). Also, the occupation of a mason.

Métro. Short for Metropolitan Railway, the name given originally to the Paris subway and now used for subways in Montreal, Washington, D.C. and other cities.

minaret. A tall slender tower attached to a mosque, from which the faithful are called to prayer.

modular. The use of standardized units (modules) for flexible arrangement and for ease in building construction.

mosaic. A surface decoration made with small pieces of stone, glass or glazed ceramic.

motif. A dominant form, shape or figure which recurs often in a design. Common in many art forms, in painting, architecture, music or literature.

mullion. A slender vertical member of stone, wood or metal between the panes of a window.

nave. The principal area of a church, extending from the main entrance to the altar area, and to the aisles or wall on each side. From the Latin word for ship, which early builders thought the nave resembled.

Neo-Classic. A trend in the architecture of Europe and America in the late 18th and early 19th centuries resulting in widespread use of Greek orders and decorative motifs.

Neo-Gothic. Revival of Gothic influences in the architecture of Europe and America in the 19th century. Found most often in the design of churches.

niche. An ornamental recess in a wall, usually meant for holding a statue or other decoration.

onyx. A translucent variety of quartz, sometimes black or jet black. Can be highly polished.

obtuse. Neither pointed nor sharp but blunted in form. An angle greater than 90 degrees.

palazzo. Italian for palace. Also for an impressive public building or an imposing residence.

parabolic. Referring to a curve made by the intersection of a plane with a right circular cone. The path of a ball thrown in an arc is a parabola.

parapet. A low protective wall or barrier at the edge of a roof.

parquet. A floor of inlaid design, usually wood or marble.

pavilion. Used sometimes in architectural nomenclature to describe a dormitory or residence hall, e.g., the Swiss Pavilion. Usually, a light open building used for concerts or shelter.

pediment. A low, gable-like feature, often triangular in design and usually placed over an entrance or doorway. In Greek architecture it often surmounts the entire facade.

Pentellic. Referring to Pentelicus, a mountain near Athens noted for its superb marble.

piazza. Italian for an open square or public place in a city or town.

pier. A vertical support in building construction. Often a pillar rectangular in cross-section.

pilaster. A pier or column set into a wall, sometimes as an ornament but usually for reinforcing.

pillar. A slender freestanding pier or column used as a vertical support in building construction.

piloti. French word for columns or stilts used to raise a structure above the ground, leaving free space below.

pinnacle. A structure capping a tower or a small spire or turret atop a roof.

Piranesi. An 18th century Italian architect and engraver.

plinth. The slab-like base on which a building stands. The square base of a pedestal.

portal. A large and impressive entrance, gate or doorway.

portico. A structure attached to a building, composed of a roof supported by columns or piers, serving as a porch.

post-and-beam. A structural system wherein two or more posts support a horizontal beam. Also called post-and-lintel.

pre-cast. Generally referring to the concrete members of a structure that have been cast in a factory and shipped to the building site.

prismatic. Resembling the varied shapes and facets of a prism.

Prix de Rome. A prize given by art and architecture juries in various countries enabling the recipient to live and study in Rome for a year or longer.

proscenium. The arch that separates the stage from the auditorium of a modern theater.

punched window. Windows separated from each other by exterior wall space, as opposed to banded windows touching each other (ribbon windows).

refectory. A dining hall in a monastery, college or other institution.

rendering. A carefully finished representation of a building exterior or interior in perspective.

Rococo. A style of architecture and design originating in France in the 18th century. Evolved from Baroque but with even more emphasis on ornamentation.

Roman brick. A long, thin brick used first by the Romans. Used often in houses by Frank Lloyd Wright.

Roman cross. Similar to the Greek cross but the vertical member is longer than the side arms.

Romanticism. An art movement originating in the late 18th century. In architecture it was a revolt against the conventional classicism of the day. In painting it emphasized strong emotion and imagination and a preference for exotic subject matter.

shed roof. A flat roof higher on one side than on the opposite.

silhouette. An outline of something that appears dark against a light background. After Etienne de Silhouette (1709–1767).

sill. The horizontal base of a window. In balloon framing, the horizontal base of a wall.

skin. In modern architecture, the thin outer wall of a building, usually of glass or thin sheets of metal. Said of buildings by Mies van der Rohe, "skin and bones."

space frame. A three-dimensional framework for enclosing space, with all parts being interconnected. Some have pyramidal elements, others are based on the hexagon or other geometric figures.

spandrel. On a building facade, the horizontal space between the bottom line of the windows and the base of that floor. Also, the space between two arches and the horizontal molding above them.

stiffened arch. A type of bridge pioneered by Robert Maillart in which thin vertical slabs of concrete rest on a concrete arch and support the roadway.

stucco. A finish for exterior walls applied wet and made of cement, sand and lime with water. Also a fine plaster for decorative interior work.

stylobate. A course of masonry forming the base for a colonnade, a row of columns.

sun baffle. A slab or grille designed to shade the interior from direct sunlight. Le Corbusier designed small ones to project horizontally above each window.

tension ring. A ring of metal or reinforced concrete, above or below the ground, which absorbs the thrust of the ribs of a dome.

tension structure. A structure similar to a tent, in which the supporting members are held in tension by cables.

tetrahedron. A geometric solid with four faces, e.g., a pyramid with three sides and a base.

tiara. An ornamental headpiece resembling a crown.

Tinian marble. Particularly fine marble quarried on the island of Tinos in the Aegean Sea.

transept. A transverse arm of the body of a cruciform church, crossing the nave in front of the choir.

trapezoid. A four-sided geometric figure having two parallel and two nonparallel sides.

travertine. A cream-colored stone used as a facing material for buildings and sometimes for floors.

truncated. Having the apex (e.g., that of a pyramid) cut off and replaced by a flat plane. A trapezoid is a truncated pyramid in outline.

truss. A rigid framework of wooden or metal beams used to support a structure, often a bridge.

truss work. A system of trusses supporting a structure.

turret. A small tower or tower-like structure projecting from a building.

Tuscan. Relating to the area of Tuscany in Italy. Also an architectural order resembling a simplified Roman Doric.

venturi. A narrowed passage causing air or other fluids flowing through it to move at greater speeds and pressures. Discovered by G.B. Venturi (1746–1822), Italian physicist.

vestibule. A small entrance hall or lobby.

Vierendeel truss. A method of stiffening exterior walls with vertical and horizontal members, as opposed to X-bracing.

INDEX

ACKNOWLEDGEMENTS

Thanks to Architect A. Richard Williams, who introduced me to many of the fine buildings in this book, to Dione Neutra for lending me the photographs of her husband's buildings, to Marie-Claire Blumer Maillart for her friendship and the book on her father's bridges, to Professor Juan Murcia Vela for the photographs of Torroja's works. Among authors who have helped by their fine books are Peter Blake, H. Allen Brooks, George R. Collins, Carl Condit, James M. Fitch, Sigfried Giedion, Ada Louise Huxtable, Esther McCoy and Vincent Scully, Jr.

Thanks also to Margaret McCandless and the editorial staff of Davis Publications, and to the staff of Milner Library, Illinois State University.